The Kemetic Tree of Life

Uncover the Secret Philosophical Teachings of the Kemetic Tree of Life and Ancient Egyptian Spirituality

© Copyright 2025 - All rights reserved.

The content contained within this book may not be reproduced, duplicated, or transmitted without direct written permission from the author or the publisher.

Under no circumstances will any blame or legal responsibility be held against the publisher or author for any damages, reparation, or monetary loss due to the information contained within this book, either directly or indirectly.

Legal Notice:

This book is copyright-protected. It is only for personal use. You cannot amend, distribute, sell, use, quote, or paraphrase any part of the content within this book without the consent of the author or publisher.

Disclaimer Notice:

Please note the information contained within this document is for educational and entertainment purposes only. All effort has been executed to present accurate, up-to-date, reliable, and complete information. No warranties of any kind are declared or implied. Readers acknowledge that the author is not engaging in the rendering of legal, financial, medical, or professional advice. The content within this book has been derived from various sources. Please consult a licensed professional before attempting any techniques outlined in this book.

By reading this document, the reader agrees that under no circumstances is the author responsible for any losses, direct or indirect, that are incurred as a result of the use of the information contained within this document, including, but not limited to, errors, omissions, or inaccuracies.

Your Free Gift
(only available for a limited time)

Thanks for getting this book! If you want to learn more about various spirituality topics, then join Mari Silva's community and get a free guided meditation MP3 for awakening your third eye. This guided meditation mp3 is designed to open and strengthen ones third eye so you can experience a higher state of consciousness. Simply visit the link below the image to get started.

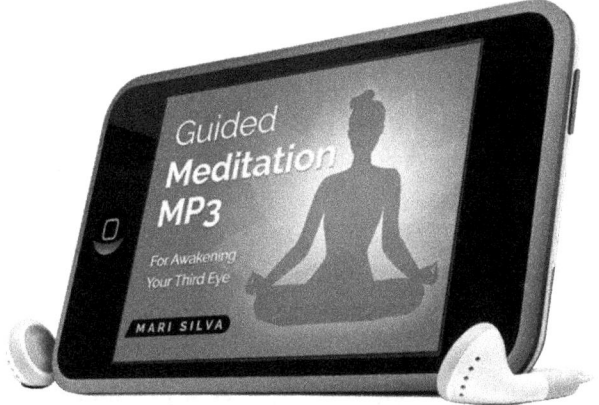

https://spiritualityspot.com/meditation
Or, Scan the QR code!

Table of Contents

INTRODUCTION 1
CHAPTER 1: THE FOUNDATIONS OF THE KEMETIC TREE OF LIFE 3
CHAPTER 2: THE NETERU SPHERES 15
CHAPTER 3: MA'AT AND THE TREE OF LIFE 27
CHAPTER 4: TREE OF LIFE NUMEROLOGY 40
CHAPTER 5: ASCENDING THE KEMETIC TREE OF LIFE 53
CHAPTER 6: THE POWER OF SACRED EGYPTIAN SYMBOLS ... 64
CHAPTER 7: THE KEMETIC TREE OF LIFE FOR PERSONAL GROWTH 76
CHAPTER 8: REAWAKENING THE TREE OF LIFE IN MODERN TIMES 91
APPENDIX: KEMETIC TREE OF LIFE GLOSSARY 103
CONCLUSION 108
HERE'S ANOTHER BOOK BY MARI SILVA THAT YOU MIGHT LIKE 111
YOUR FREE GIFT (ONLY AVAILABLE FOR A LIMITED TIME) ... 112
REFERENCES 113
IMAGE SOURCES 121

Introduction

Rooted in the symbolism of ancient cultures, the Tree of Life is a mysterious yet incredibly powerful device. When aligned with its energies, the Tree shows the interconnectedness of everything in nature and the universe. It also serves as a reminder that the universe is far bigger than what people can consciously perceive and that there are plenty of hidden nooks and crannies to explore by reaching beyond the conscious. For the same reason, the Tree of Life is a symbol sought after by many spiritual seekers who wish to unveil connections, universal truths, and collective wisdom gathered through age-old energies.

This book will provide a thorough introduction to the origins and inner workings of the Tree of Life, taking a deep dive into its role in ancient Egyptian culture, as well as a spiritual guide for past and modern practitioners. It discusses its symbolism through different lenses, including numerological and transformational, along with its potential to restore harmony on individual, communal, and even global levels.

However, make no mistake, this isn't just another book about the history and practices surrounding the Tree of Life. Unlike others in the same category, this book provides a simplified explanation of all the relevant concepts related to the Kemetic Tree of Life. Even if you're a complete newcomer to the topic and have no previous knowledge or understanding of the Tree's symbolism, you'll have no trouble navigating the pages of this book.

This book also offers unique historical insights, fostering a deeper appreciation of the Tree's role in Egyptian spirituality and culture. As one of the most prominent guiding forces in Egyptian spiritual beliefs and practices, the principles of the Tree of Life are deeply interwoven into the practitioners' lives. Understanding the symbolism that ties the Tree to this belief system will provide you with a more well-rounded picture of the spiritual tool you'll learn about in this book.

Another aspect that sets this book apart from all the others in the market is the abundance of practical exercises, tips, and advice for integrating the Tree into various aspects of spiritual practices. In each chapter, you'll find at least one easy-to-follow exercise designed with beginners in mind but also suitable for a little more experienced practitioners.

From meditation to rituals to various forms of reflection exercises, you won't have trouble finding ways to work with the Tree of Life. Each one is designed to cover a specific aspect of the Tree, helping you apply its teachings to enhance your life and induce spiritual growth. If you're ready to embark on this transformational journey and start harnessing the Tree's wisdom, all you have to do is continue reading.

Chapter 1: The Foundations of the Kemetic Tree of Life

In ancient Egyptian culture, the Kemetic Tree of Life is recognized today as more of a symbol than an actual tree. It's not one image but many connected to spiritual figures and hieroglyphs. The symbolic tree represents philosophical teachings and the profound principles of Ma'at. It's a sacred symbol of ancient Egyptian, or Kemetic, culture encompassing the cosmic order that creates a balanced, harmonious universe. It laid the groundwork for the patterns adopted by the scientific community to understand the universal order and how these are intertwined in the soul's journey. Often stylized in depictions, the Kemetic tree's symbolism is far more grounded than one would think and can be used as a guide for personal growth.

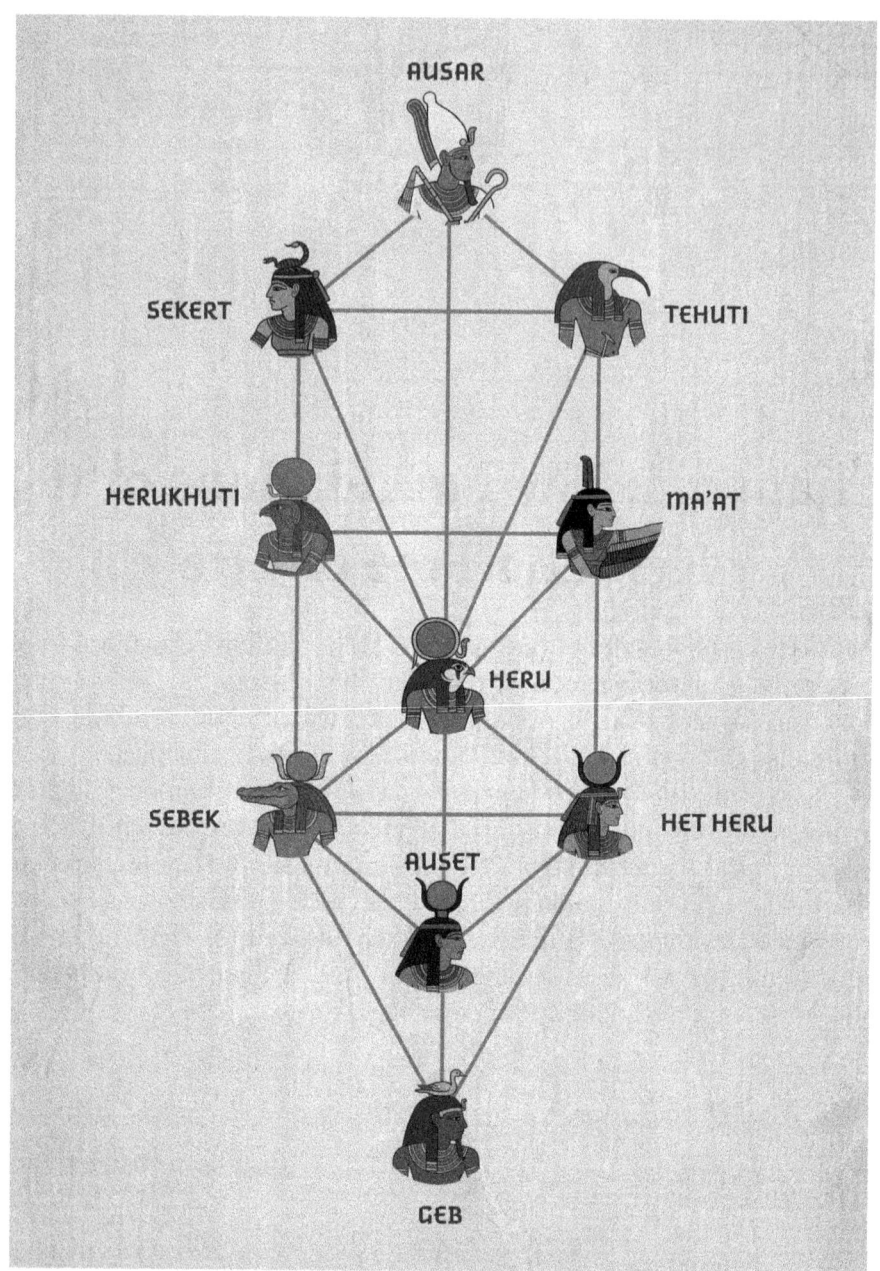

In this chapter, you will learn the foundations of the Kemetic Tree of Life, its significance, origins, and key principles derived from myth. You will discover the wisdom of ancient Egyptian spirituality and how it applies today. You will also find a guide and practice exercise to encourage your own spiritual evolution.

The Significance of the Kemetic Tree of Life

The Ancient Egyptian Worldview and the Connection Between Spirituality, Philosophy, and Daily Life

The significance of the Kemetic Tree of Life is the belief that there is a profound connection between spirituality, philosophy, and daily life, and this intriguing path is available to anyone who integrates with Kemetic spirituality. The Kemetic people engaged in philosophical practices in honor of the tree, believing its wisdom transcended earth and connected life to a higher power.

The ancient Egyptians' worldview was that spirituality flows through every aspect of existence and that the temples and everything surrounding them all have a soul. Every animal, object, and building has a spirit infused with Kemetic magic. The people were anchored in the belief that the gods were given responsibilities to rule over different aspects of life and provided gifts to society, representing the interconnectedness of systems.

The gods and goddesses believed the meaning of this tree was the combination of conscious existence and objective reality and that they were immortalized through performing daily rituals in honor of the tree. The tree implied there was an afterlife and symbolized eternal life, divinity, and creation, where the gods obtained eternal youth. Ordinary people came to learn that good deeds on earth were rewarded in this postmortem realm, that they would be protected from evil forces thanks to Kemetic spirituality, and that divinity and eternity weren't limited to superior beings. They understood that the tree's power could grant them endless possibilities, from connecting to their inner divinity and higher powers to achieving immortality in heaven.

At its core, Kemetic spirituality represents living in harmony with Ma'at. The tree symbolizes the cosmic ceremony that is order, balance, and truth. Kemetic principles., such as valuing the connection between humanity and the divine., have guided ancient Egyptian society and individuals. These principles are ones to live by today. The ancient Egyptians' philosophical and spiritual motifs apply to modern life. Their journeys lay the blueprint for future generations regarding the importance of legacy, culture, symbolic representations, and appreciation for the natural world.

The simplest meaning of the Tree of Life is creation, that of wisdom, guidance, and connection. It embodies how the physical reality of earth is created from energy, and people are imbued with spiritual meaning. The Tree of Life symbolizes the manifestations of reality, how it reaches its full potential in the cosmic order, and how everything functions together through the laws of nature and the unity of the universe.

According to myth, four sycamore trees were created to identify the four corners of the world, and the fifth and final tree was created to mark the center of the universe, linking them together. It was called the Tree of Life. They represented different aspects of life, such as knowledge, fertility, beauty, truthfulness, and justice. Every god and goddess ruled over a corner tree. Osiris was associated with the eastern sycamore tree in Egypt, and the one in the west was ruled by Hathor.

The central sycamore tree is referred to as the Kemetic Tree of Life as it connects the paths to the four parts of the world. Ptah, the creator god, ruled over it and ensured people could safely travel through Egypt without encountering dangers.

The world pillar is another mythic motif derived from the Egyptian tree, along with the world tree and axis mundi concepts. This symbol represents order, unity, and stability in Egyptian mythology and is depicted as a stone column that is so tall that it connects heaven and earth, the highest and lowest realms, from the sky to the underworld. The philosophy behind this is that the world tree maintains balance and order in the universe, ensuring harmony between every living thing. Ancient Egyptian culture believed this world pillar represented all life and that society would succumb to chaos and disorder without it, so they worshipped the tree to ensure prosperity. This world pillar didn't just inspire generations spiritually and philosophically. It has impacted all areas of growth, with architects using it to feature the durability and strength of their buildings.

The Symbolic and Visual Structure of the Kemetic Tree of Life

The symbolic structure of the Tree of Life has been repeatedly depicted in art and literature and is associated with bringing new life into the world every day. Egyptian myth has engulfed generations, with people from all over the world associating this world tree with the sun God Ra, as the father or king of the Egyptian gods, who granted this tree to symbolize ever-lasting creation in the universe, proving life is inevitable. The visual structure of the tree represents rays of sunlight in honor of the sun god. Each branch is a metaphor for the branches of the Nile River.

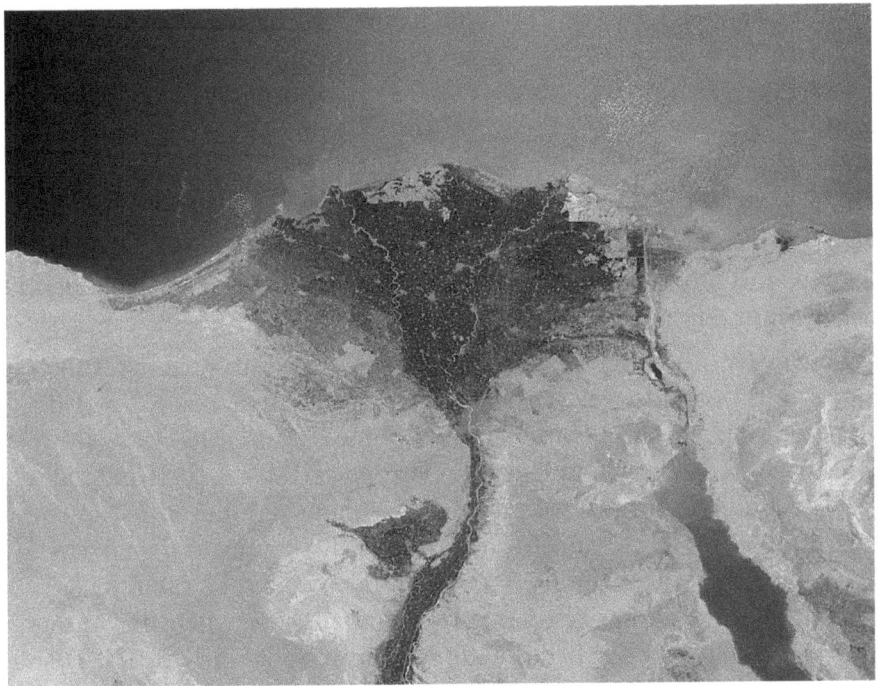

Each branch in the Kemetic Tree of Life mirrors the Nile River's branches.[1]

The cosmic structure of the tree is not only rooted in Egyptian philosophy and mythology but also establishes the cosmological framework in which all living things can be described. It offers a profound and nuanced perspective on the human experience, creativity, and interconnectedness of life. Modern understanding of the complexity of systems in the universe has been revolutionized by the concept of the world pillar.

The Tree of Life has helped the world understand the hierarchical structure of Earth, Heaven, and the Underworld. Whether you believe in the divine creator, higher powers, or a scientific structure that works in tandem to create the universe, it is because of the world pillar that people understand the universe's formula.

The Parallels of the Tree of Life to Sacred Geometry and the Interconnectedness of All Life

Much like sacred geometry, the Tree of Life structure represents the fundamental blueprint of creation. It reveals the organization and harmony of energy through patterns understood by a mathematical language, proving that the world operates through precise, interconnected relationships. You can track these relationships through the consistent patterns observed in nature, art, architecture, and your own cells. The symbolic structure of the tree illuminates the architecture of reality, underlying all existence and demonstrating the coherence of creation.

Just like sacred geometry explains the cohesive orchestration of all existence, the Tree of Life structure bridges the same belief, the perfect balance of science and intuition, and the ability to create wondrous, ethereal, and other-worldly designs and insights that can be explained by analytics and rationality.

This proves the Tree of Life design is not random or a byproduct of chance and coincidence. It speaks to an order that resonates with all living things, like the fundamental seed of life that grew to create flowers, plants, trees, etc. Just looking at the pure perfection of the Kemetic tree structure provides a sense of recognition, understanding, consciousness, and wonder. It allows one to acknowledge that universal patterns are everywhere, including within you, as an artist, painter, spiritual seeker, or dancer. There is an intuitive response humans have when they connect to the sacred tree. They become aware and emboldened by the cosmic interconnections, curiosity, and exploration of nature's principles. It allows them to embrace their own transformation and changing perceptions of the world since every living thing is connected and created by these intricate patterns. It all begins with the clearest sign of nature's creation: the Kemetic Tree of Life, the enduring symbol of hope and rebirth.

The concept of interconnectedness in Egyptian mythology relates to symbols of life and immortality, like the Ankh. They believed that connecting with people and nature brought fulfillment and spiritual enlightenment. Kemetic people used ritualistic practices like prayer and meditation to understand their souls and those around them. This belief shaped their culture, emphasizing creating peaceful surroundings rather than fighting to conquer them.

Origins and Key Principles of the Tree of Life in Ancient Egyptian Spirituality

The Emergence of the Tree of Life Concept in Kemetic Culture

The Kemetic Tree of Life symbol originated in the Nile Valley Civilization of ancient Egypt, modeled after the large sycamore tree in the center of the world. It represents the spiritual and hierarchical system that creates the chain of events that brings everything to life. It symbolizes the existence of every atom and galaxy, with the tree's roots connecting all living things and worlds through energy.

The divine gods relied on the tree to travel between realms, and people believed it would ascend their souls to heaven or descend them into hell based on how well they honored the principles of the tree, meaning how well they appeased the creator god. The sycamore tree was the definitive representation of Egypt due to being the sturdiest and largest. In religion, it was believed that this was the one tree that symbolizes life and death, the order, process, and method of creation, because it grew at the edge of deserts and near necropolises.

This powerful and sacred tree held all layers of existence together, maintaining consistency and balance in the universe. So, to honor the tree's principles, people would seek knowledge to improve their own lives and respect the intricacies of the universe and what gave them life. They would cherish their own lives as gifts from the tree of creation and focused on finding their purpose to live righteously.

The Tree of Life concept first emerged in Kemetic culture through the story of the original duo or team of the universe: the sky and the earth. The two realms were the first two spheres of the tree derived from the Acacia tree of Iusaaset according to the ancient Egyptians. This made trees sacred in ancient Egypt, as there weren't many. The myth then evolved as all these spheres were found to be a part of the largest and most majestic tree in the land, known in Egyptian folklore as the Tree of Life.

Pharaohs enhanced the key principles of the Tree in Kemetic culture as they were considered the descendants of the sun god Ra, the creator. The various spheres connected to the majestic tree proved there were more realms represented by the tree than earth and heaven, and the pharaohs were given superior powers by taking responsibility for each sphere that connected two main dimensions: the spiritual and the physical. Their goal was to rule over important elements of life and each corner of the world to help maintain universal balance.

The Egyptian Tree of Life symbolized it all, the mythic and visual representation of this grand connection, bringing ordinary people closer to spiritual beings. The tree's branches were a reminder to ordinary people to believe in the tree's principles and that they would become one with the creator and gods themselves, living in eternal peace and happiness with the others.

The Kemetic Tree's Role in Ancient Cosmology

The Kemetic tree had a vital role in ancient cosmology. It provided the understanding that all life emerges from one source and features the multiple spheres that sustain life on Earth. The ancient Egyptian approach to metaphysics and higher consciousness through the structure of the Tree of Life has expanded into modern wisdom, believing the origins of the universe were an abyss until the birth of the Tree of Life. It is scientifically known as the Big Bang, which created the cosmological blueprint that explains the concept of harmony and balance. It allows the tradition of spirituality to explain and flourish in the modern world.

The Tree of Life Philosophy in Ancient Texts

Ancient Egyptian texts include the philosophy relevant to the Tree of Life. For example, the Tree of Life resurrected the king in the Pyramid texts. The Egyptian Book of the Dead also highlights the tree's power to preserve life, including prayers, hymns, and maps to guide and help the soul navigate the underworld. The deceased and deities were given a second chance in the afterlife, and these texts described the journey in the postmortem territory and the different paths and gates one would come across.

The journey would be challenging, and gods would have to help them overcome obstacles. To call upon these gods for guidance, they'd need the knowledge of magical spells. These concepts require the same knowledge to enlist the tree's powers, from the help of gods to guide them into altered states of consciousness and retrieve their souls. They'd have to live their life with honor, emphasizing the willingness to grow through personal experience to achieve the afterlife. Both the Tree of Life and the Book of the Dead's philosophy indicate the transitional periods one must go through to meet their destiny in the heavenly world.

Symbolic Significance as a Representation of Universal Order

The Tree of Life's Representation of Ma'at and the Interdependence of All Aspects of Existence

The sacred tree represents the cosmic order and justice, known as *Ma'at*. Ma'at is the foundation of the tree's philosophy, embodying justice, order, truth, and an ever-lasting balance in the universe. While many discuss the wisdom of Ma'at as principles to live by, it is often depicted as a goddess who was the vital component of the world's stability. The Egyptian people had to adhere to her teachings to ensure happiness in their own lives if they wanted to align with the cosmic order.

Ma'at.²

The Tree of Life represents Ma'at by emphasizing the interdependence of all aspects of existence, providing a wealth of knowledge to help one align with the natural world. The Egyptians believed that Ma'at was upheld by the gods through the Tree of Life to maintain stability in the universe. They believed that all life was interwoven with nature through the tree's power, so if the tree was not respected and taken care of, the world would collapse with it.

The political and religious leader, the pharaoh, represented the gods and was entrusted to nurture Ma'at by encouraging living in peace and honoring the cosmic principles of stability, veracity, and structure. The Tree of Life remained the physical essence of these principles, reflecting their culture, and it was a reminder to the ancient Egyptians to maintain these principles in their personal lives for the betterment of society. It guided them to live by these values if they wanted to maintain the connection between the human and divine realms.

Key Myths Reflecting the Values Encoded in the Tree of Life

Certain stories in Egyptian mythology have integrated modern culture to pass on moral lessons reflecting the beliefs birthed by the Tree of Life. The following myths offer insight into the themes of death, resurrection, the afterlife, and the values of order and balance. These legends are central to Kemetic culture, exemplifying and revolving around the importance of the Tree of Life's philosophy and divine motifs.

- **Osiris**

Osiris was the god of the dead and the afterlife and the first ruler of the world. After being murdered by his wicked brother Set out of jealousy for his power, his wife Isis resurrected him. Acts of piety granted Osiris the opportunity to be reborn.

- **Isis**

Osiris' wife-and sister-Isis, found a chest that had traveled down the river Nile and brought it to a tamarisk tree to preserve her husband's corpse, an act of reverence to the divine creation of life. The tree grew and encircled Osiris and the chest within its trunk. The tree's branches reached out, representing the axis mundi, holding up the heavens, making it the pillar of Egyptian mythology - the epitome of life's cycle of birth, growth, death, and renewal.

- **Horus**

The son of Osiris became the leader of the living after avenging his father's death, fulfilling the duties one should have on Earth to sustain the cosmic order of life and reach the afterlife. He epitomized the Tree of Life's values by following through on moral obligations, which are fundamental in Egyptian religious practice.

These myths tell the story of the Kemetic people's belief in the afterlife. They constructed elaborate monumental tombs, like the pyramids, and partook in burial rituals to manifest their ascension into the spiritual realm. They would preserve corpses to ensure they were sent to the afterlife safely and granted eternal existence by the gods. The emphasis of these myths reinforced the belief that the nature of life is cyclical, as is death and the promise of rebirth.

A Guide to Spiritual Evolution

The Tree of Life can be a guide for spiritual evolution and self-realization. It symbolizes the cycle of creation established and sustained by divine forces. These forces or energies embody the transformations all living things do, going from birth to death and rebirth. This doesn't just apply to life and death specifically but also to how one changes throughout one's lifetime and how one part of you must shed to start anew, like a snake's skin. Think of the caterpillar who goes through a transformation similar to death and is reborn as a butterfly, ready for the next stage of life. Through this wisdom, you can learn to evolve and reach enlightenment by accepting the sacrifices made along the way and the rewards you'll reap as a result. Understanding the forces that govern your existence can help you honor them and achieve life fulfillment.

The divine energies or forces that uphold these universal principles were called Neteru by the Egyptians. They were manifestations of the universe's cyclical nature and their relationship to the Tree of Life is what quite literally makes the world go around. In the Kemetic language, the word Neter means god, self-created one, or power. These gods and goddesses are gifted cosmic forces, ensuring all elements of creation are generated by the birth, death, and renewal cycle.

Without the Tree of Life, this system would never have amounted to more than a mythic tale. Neteru is responsible for different aspects of the universe by maintaining the order of the Tree of Life. Therefore, the Tree of Life can help you on your spiritual path. You can apply these structures on your personal growth journey, maintaining a healthy balance in your life, making sacrifices for the greater good, understanding concepts like creation, honor, and love, and overcoming obstacles by understanding that you're simply approaching the rebirth stage. Even if you lose something along the way, it is Neteru's way of making room for what you will gain in the future. Through meditation, prayer, or creating a small altar to worship the gods, you can show your respect and appreciation for the gift of life and ask for support and guidance to live pleasantly within the Kemetic Tree's order.

The philosophical teachings explained above remain relevant in addressing modern spiritual, ethical, and existential questions. The Tree of Life can be a tool for understanding yourself, others, and the universe. You can nourish a connection with the people around you and your ancestors who have reached the heavens and enrich your personal beliefs through the spirituality of the Kemetic Tree of Life. By maintaining a personal connection to the divine forces, you will understand where you are in life, where you want to be, how to get there, and how to help others. You'll also discover how to live in an ethical way to achieve successful experiences of transformation, knowing that no matter what you've been through, there's always a chance for rebirth.

Practical Exercise

Connect with the Tree of Life (Meditation):

1. Find a peaceful space where you can pray or meditate. If you have set up a small altar, you can use this space to spiritually connect to the Tree of Life.
2. Visualize the Kemetic Tree of Life as a glowing structure connecting the heavens, earth, and the underworld like an orb that surrounds the realms with its branches conjoining them.
3. Sit quietly and focus on your breath. Imagine energy flowing through the tree into your body, with each soft breath in and out grounding and balancing you.
4. You can end the meditation by expressing gratitude to the tree for its wisdom, support, and vibrant energy.

In the chapters to come, you will discover even more about the Neteru forces, the principles of Ma'at, and practical exercises to help you connect with the Kemetic Tree of Life and gain support on your spiritual journey.

Chapter 2: The Neteru Spheres

Every ancient culture has its own deities. The Norse had Thor and Loki, the Greeks had Poseidon and Aphrodite, and the Romans had Venus and Mars. People have been telling their stories for centuries, and the fascination has never ceased. Ancient Egyptian deities, or the Neteru, have some of the most interesting mythology in history. They also play a major role in Kemetic spirituality and the Tree of Life.

Ancient Egyptian deities, or the Neteru, have some of the most interesting mythology in history.[3]

This chapter explores the nature and significance of the Neteru with their myths, symbolism, and key deities relating to the Tree.

What Is the Neteru?

The Neteru are ancient Egyptian deities embodying divine energy or principles, forces of nature, and aspects of the divine essence. According to ancient Egyptian mythology, they played a role in the creation cycle. Like all creatures, these forces go through the stages of life: birth, aging, death, and rebirth.

The world goes through different cycles, such as seasonal changes and day and night. The Neteru are the forces of nature that maintain balance in the universe and keep it running. Calling them just gods or goddesses is an understatement.

The Neteru are responsible for the creation cycle. Understanding them and their role in the existence of the universe requires not seeing them as one entity but as male and female energies working together.

The ancient Egyptians called the male Neteru "Neter," meaning "nature or a power that creates and maintains life." The female is called "Netert." Since they undergo the same cycle of transformation as all beings, they are believed to be born or created and undergo various changes, similar to aging, until they cease to exist (die) and are recreated in a different form (rebirth).

For instance, the caterpillar is born, grows, builds a cocoon, dies in it, and is reborn into a butterfly that lays eggs and continues the cycle. The Neteru go through a similar process and transform from one energy form to another.

Viewing the Neteru as energy forces instead of just deities can help you understand the Ancient Egyptian system and how it works.

The Dual Roles and Psychological Archetypes

Swedish psychologist Carl Jung coined the term "Archetype," meaning what can manifest from one's collective unconscious. This refers to the human experience that one inherits from ancestral memory or a higher power. The collective unconscious encompasses all potential experiences and lives. It can also be a timeline of the universe that shows the future, present, and the past before time and space.

In physics, the invisible world is called the "microcosm," and the visible world is called the "macrocosm." People are aware of the macrocosm and live in it. However, the microcosm is invisible and unpredictable and can impact every aspect of one's life. This applies to the conscious and unconscious mind. You notice your thoughts and emotions that stem from your unconscious. When they are brought to the conscious mind, they can affect you in different ways.

The macrocosm is also defined as the cosmos with its planets, stars, galaxies, etc. It is larger and more complex than the human mind can comprehend. The microcosm is a small part of it, representing mankind and their experiences. It is believed that the universe is a living being, and all people's actions are a reflection of it.

Both the macrocosm and the microcosm represent the relationships between the individual and the universe. Both are interconnected and governed by the same principles.

Psychological archetypes exist in the microcosm within individuals. While some of these archetypes live and breathe in the real world, others remain in the subconscious and can never be explained. However, they are open to interpretation, with each culture creating its own and giving it different characteristics and stories.

For instance, the ancient Egyptians had Horus, the Hindu culture has Krishna, and the Christians have Jesus. While all these archetypes represent the Divine Child, their portrayals differ. Horus's archetypal Mother figure was Isis, while Jesus had Mary. Horus and Krishna had uncles who stirred trouble. These evil individuals represent the shadow side of the archetypal divine father. Each story provides a different interpretation of how Horus and Krishna defeated their uncles and took their rightful place on the throne.

Key Figures in Ancient Egypt

This part explores the most significant deities in ancient Egypt.

Ra

Ra was the sun god and the creator. He was the supreme deity in ancient Egypt and represented light, power, kingship, and heaven. In some legends, he was believed to be the sun itself. He would ride across the heavens during the day and rest in the underworld in the evening, all through the night until sunrise.

Every night, a giant and evil serpent named Apep or Apophis fought Ra to stop the sun from rising to kill all living creatures. However, Ra was always victorious. Richard H. Wilkinson and other archaeologists and scholars agree that Ra is the most prominent deity in ancient Egypt. He not only embodied the sun's power, but he also created other gods and goddesses who shaped ancient Egyptian mythology.

Ra.'

Ra was known as the "Self-Created-One" because nothing and no one created him. He emerged from the waters of chaos to create the universe, establish order, and give birth to other deities.

Before the creation of the universe, there was only water and dry land where Ra stood. He cut his penis and used the blood to create Sia (the mind) and Hu (authority). Soon after, Ra realized he was alone, so he mated with his shadow and gave birth to Tefnut, the goddess of moisture, and Shu, the god of the air. He sent them to finish creating the universe.

However, Tefnut and Shu didn't return, so Ra sent the Eye of Ra to bring them. When his children returned home, Ra was pleased and cried tears of joy. They fell on dry land and created men and women. Shu and Tefnut realized that these new creatures didn't have a place to live. They mated and gave birth to Nut, the goddess of the sky, and Geb, the god of the earth, who also mated and gave birth to some of the most significant deities in ancient Egyptian mythology: Osiris, Isis, Set, Nephthys, and Horus the elder.

Each deity had its own sphere of influence to keep the balance and maintain order in the universe.

Ra had different representations when combined with other gods. When he was one with Amun, the god of the air, he was known as Amun-Ra. He became the patron of the sun and symbolized its eternal power.

He was also combined with Horus and was called "Ra-Horakhty," meaning "Ra-Horus in the horizon." Horus was the human form of Ra and ruled over ancient Egypt for years. Ra also transformed into his daughters Hathor, the goddess of pleasure, dancing, beauty, music, and love, and Sekhmet, the goddess of war, chaos, and plague.

Osiris

Osiris was the god of the dead and the underworld and ruled over the afterlife. He was Geb and Nut's oldest son. The name "Osiris" was derived from "Usir," meaning "the mighty." Before his association with death, Osiris was depicted as a handsome young prince wearing Upper Egypt's crown and holding symbols of royalty, such as the crook and flail. However, later, he was depicted as a mummy.

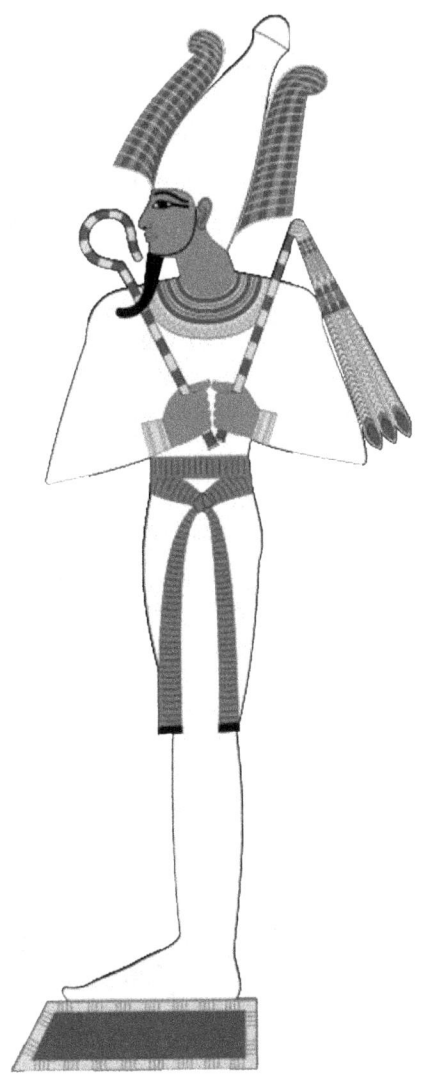

Osiris.[5]

Since he died and was brought back to life, he became associated with the mythical Bennu bird, which was the ancient Egyptian version of the Phoenix.

Osiris had many names, but the most popular ones were "Khenti Amenti," meaning "the Foremost of the Westerners," which symbolized his role as the Judge of the Dead. In ancient Egypt, death was associated with the West, and Westerners represented those who crossed over to the other side. He was also called "*Wennefer,*" meaning "the beautiful one."

Before his death and descent to the underworld, Osiris was called the Eternal Lord, King of the Living, and the Lord of Love. Osiris is the perfect example of duality. He was portrayed as a generous, kind, just, and giving god, and also a terrifying deity who sent his demon messengers after the living to bring them to the underworld.

Osiris was the first king of Egypt, and he developed the rules and values all the kings who came after him followed. Ancient Egyptians were mummified to look like Osiris to drive away evil spirits.

All the kings who came after him copied his appearance. They were depicted holding a staff and flail, showing the Osiris influence on Ancient Egypt's culture and its pharaohs.

Isis

Isis was the goddess of magic and healing and was considered the Great Mother. The name Isis was Greek. "Aset" was her Egyptian name, meaning "the Queen of the Throne." It was derived from "Eset," meaning "Seat," symbolizing the throne and stability. Isis was King Horus's mother and came to be known as the mother of every pharaoh.

Isis.[6]

She was one of the most important goddesses in ancient Egypt and was considered the bringer of magic and the protector of women. Isis symbolized the cosmic order and was believed to be the queen of the universe and the controller of fate.

Isis had many symbols, such as the sistrum (an Ancient Egyptian musical instrument), an empty throne (symbolizing her husband's untimely death and leaving his throne), a kite (a type of falcon that she transformed into when she brought Osiris to life), and the scorpion (which protected her when she was hiding from her brother Set).

Isis was a selfless and generous protectress, mother, and wife, and put everyone's needs before hers. She was also called "*Mut-Netjer,*" meaning "Mother of the Gods," and "*Weret-Hekau*," meaning "The Great Magic." She was called *Ankhet* for creating and preserving life, and she made the Nile flood every year, allowing farmers to fertilize their lands.

Over time, Isis was the most popular goddess in ancient Egypt and was the only deity every Egyptian worshiped. They built a temple in her honor and used it to worship her, pray for her, and make offerings, but only the high priestesses were allowed inside. She was even worshiped in Greece and Rome.

Set

Set, Seth, or Suetekh, was the god of earthquakes, eclipses, thunderstorms, war, chaos, disorder, foreign lands, and deserts. His name means the destroyer or instigator of confusion. Unlike his siblings, Orisis and Isis, he was frightening and powerful, but he used his power for evil. However, he protected the spirits of the dead on their journey to the Afterlife. He also protected his great-grandfather Ra from the chaos serpent Apophis, which attacked Ra every night to prevent the sun from rising.

During the Early Dynastic Period of Egypt, Set was a heroic figure. When Apophis hypnotized Ra, Set resisted and attacked him with a great spear. As a result, he played a role in the sun rising every morning and protected all life on Earth. In Upper Egypt, people inscribed his name on amulets to create love charms and invoked him for love spells.

However, during the New Kingdom, he was known as a murderer, especially when the Osiris myth spread across ancient Egypt. No one knows why ancient Egyptians transformed Set from a hero and protector into a murderer and a lover of chaos. Even though his reputation was tarnished, pharaohs and peasants would invoke him and pray for his assistance.

Set.[7]

However, he remained a villain in Ancient Egyptian mythology, representing invasion, hunger, destruction, famine, doubt, waste, chaos, and everything the Egyptians feared and hated.

The Connection Between the Neteru and the Kemetic Tree of Life

The Neteru aren't merely deities but are viewed as archetype energies that exist within individuals. Each Neter symbolizes characteristics from the divine, such as power, love, and wisdom. Ancient Egyptians worked with these energies for spiritual practice.

In ancient Egyptian mythology, death isn't the end of one's journey. They continue existing as spirits in the Afterlife. Only the bodies perish, while Ka (the soul) never dies and undergoes trials to determine whether it has led an honest or dishonest life. So, what is the role of the Kemetic Tree of Life? Well, its teachings prepare the soul for the journey and help it navigate the Afterlife.

The Kemetic Tree of Life consists of 11 spheres, from sphere zero, which is at the top of the tree, to sphere ten.

- **Sphere Zero:** It is the invisible divine nature of mankind. Amun-Ra, the king of gods, represents this aspect of the individual that can't be destroyed or created. It is the source of consciousness and life.
- **Sphere One:** It symbolizes the divine self of mankind and its true nature. Osiris represents this sphere.
- **Sphere Two:** Tehuti, the spiritual master, represents this sphere, which is the source of divine wisdom.
- **Sphere Three:** It is the source of life, and Sokar, the god of the dead, represents this sphere.
- **Sphere Four:** Maat, goddess of justice, rules over this sphere. It represents truth, justice, and the Divine's laws.
- **Sphere Five:** Herukhuti or Ra-Horakhty represents this sphere. It involves enforcing the Divine's karma, truth, justice, and laws.
- **Sphere Six:** Horus, the god of kingship, represents this sphere. It is the manifestation of one's will.

- **Sphere Seven:** Also represented by Horus, and is the manifestation of one's imagination.
- **Sphere Eight:** Sobek, the crocodile god, represents this sphere. It is the manifestation of one's emotions.
- **Sphere Nine:** Auset or Isis represents this sphere. It is the manifestation of motherly love.
- **Sphere Ten:** Geb represents this sphere. It is the manifestation of the Earth in the universe and the center of the individual's consciousness.

The Kemetic Tree of Life represents the relationship between the Neteru as forces of the divine and mankind. The individual's purpose stems from sphere six, which represents one's true will. Each person has free will and can make their own choices. You can follow the Divine's rules or reject them.

The individual's actions, reactions, and behavior depend on their choices. You can either work on your higher self with the Divine qualities of the Neteru spheres or focus on the lower self, which is the dysfunctional and undisciplined part of oneself.

Harmony and Balance Between Oppositional Forces

Life has no meaning without death; creation only comes after destruction, and you can only establish order when there is chaos. While opposite forces go against one another, they create balance and harmony in the universe.

Death teaches you to appreciate life. If you live forever, you will take everything for granted, including your loved ones. While many people fear death and see it as an enemy, it allows you to live and enjoy your life. You recognize its fragility and how your time is precious. As a result, you will have the courage to chase your goals, tell your loved ones how you feel about them, and live life to the fullest. So when death comes, you welcome it like a good sleep after a long and enjoyable journey.

One also needs chaos and order to grow. Chaos disrupts your life and pushes you out of your comfort zone. This forces you to adapt or make adjustments to change and evolve. Chaos challenges you to take risks and learn new things. Life without chaos is boring and will prevent you from moving forward.

Order gives you a sense of discipline, stability, security, and structure. Without it, life can become difficult and overwhelming. A chaotic life can cause anxiety, and too much order can make life rigid and dull. You need to find balance. Strive for order and creation, but welcome moments of chaos and destruction as they are inevitable. Instead of avoiding them, live through the experience and allow it to change your perspective, teach you new skills, and help you grow.

The Story of Osiris, Isis, and Horus

The ancient Egyptian story of Osiris, Isis, and Horus represents how archetypes are manifested in the microcosm and their relationship with individuals.

According to ancient Egyptian mythology, Isis and Osiris were siblings and husband and wife. Their love story is one for the ages. It is believed that they were in love since they were in the womb.

Ancient Egypt was called "Kemet," meaning "the black land," since it was a dark place where demonic forces and injustice ruled. As the firstborn, Osiris became the Lord of the Earth, and Isis was the queen. The ancient Egyptians didn't have laws or rules to govern them and were extremely uncivilized. Osiris taught them agriculture and gave them religion, culture, and laws.

The country thrived under Osiris' rule. People lived as equals, and no one was poor or hungry. There was enough food and water for everyone. All people and gods loved Osiris, except for his brother Set. Set represented chaos and destruction, while Osiris represented order and creation.

Set was jealous of what his brother accomplished and his growing popularity. The situation became worse when his wife and sister, Nephthys, disguised herself as Isis, mated with Osiris, and became pregnant with his child.

Set was furious and wanted vengeance. He built a coffin that would only fit his brother. He threw a party and told his guests he would give the box as a gift to whoever fit in it. Once Osiris entered the coffin, Set closed it shut and threw it in the Nile.

Isis was distraught but was determined to find him. She used her magic, which led her to his dead body, brought it back, and hid it from Set. Isis went to collect herbs to create a spell that would bring him back to life. She asked her sister Nephthys to protect him until she returned.

However, Set discovers Isis's plan and tricks Nephthys into revealing Osiris's location. Set cut his brother to pieces and scattered them all over ancient Egypt, on land, and in the water.

Isis was shocked to learn what happened to her beloved husband. She decided to look for all the pieces to perform her spell. Nephthys felt guilty for betraying her sister, so he helped her find his remains. Luckily, she found all the pieces and brought him back to life. She transformed into a kite, flew around him, took a seed from his body into her own, and became pregnant with their son, Horus.

Osiris, however, was missing his penis. That made him incomplete and unfit to rule Egypt. He retreated to the lands of the dead to become the god of the underworld and the Judge of the Dead.

Isis wanted to protect her son from Set, fearing that he might meet the same fate as his father. She kept him hidden until he grew up into a powerful warrior. He battled Set to win back his father's throne. In one legend, he defeated Set and cast him out. In another, he killed him.

While Set is the villain of this story, his archetype is necessary. If he hadn't unleashed chaos, Horus wouldn't have grown up to be a strong and determined warrior driven to win back what was rightfully his. He might have become a spoiled prince who was handed everything on a silver platter, and he wouldn't have appreciated his kingdom. Losing his father and his kingdom challenged and forced him to grow. Instead of inheriting the throne, he fought for it, giving him an appreciation of his unique position.

Chaos is necessary and has its place in the divine order. However, sooner or later, it will be balanced with order.

In this story, Isis and Osiris represent the divine union, while Set and Nephthys are their shadow side. However, Nephthys has a dual personality. While she allows Set to pursue his evil plans, she loves him sincerely and helps her sister find Osiris.

When Osiris ruled Egypt, everything was perfect. This didn't leave room for change or growth. Set had to create chaos, making Horus the new and younger ruler. This divine child restored order and brought a new vision to his kingdom, creating a new era and allowing the country to grow and prosper.

Ra's Daily Journey

After giving up his throne to his son Orisis, Ra returned to the heavens and spent his time as the sun god. Every day, he sailed across the sky, providing warmth, light, and life to all living beings.

In the morning, he transformed into Khepri, god of the sun, rebirth and resurrection, and another aspect of Ra. He is depicted as a scarab beetle. In the afternoon, he transforms back into Ra, who is depicted as a young man. At sunset, he became Atum, the god of the universe and another aspect of Ra. He was depicted as an old man with a cane.

Ra died every sunset when Nut, god of the sky, swallowed him. He went to the underworld and was reborn as Khepri. While in the underworld, he fought off Apophis with other gods to prevent chaos.

Ra's daily journey symbolizes the cycles of life, renewal, and protection against chaos.

Practical Exercises

Aligning with the Neteru of the Tree

Research the deities associated with the branches or aspects of the Kemetic Tree of Life. Choose one to connect with, offering a short prayer or meditation to align with that deity's attributes (e.g., wisdom, protection, creativity). For instance, you can say, "I pray that you fill me with your wisdom to make better decisions and grow into the best version of myself." Keep a journal to reflect on how the deity's energy manifests in your life.

Tree of Life Ritual for Guidance

Light a candle, sit before a drawn or printed image of the Kemetic Tree of Life, and ask it for guidance in an area of their life. Focus on a specific aspect of the tree (e.g., the roots for grounding, the branches for inspiration, etc.). Sit in silence, listen for intuitive messages, and write them down afterward.

_____

_____

_____

The Neteru sphere may seem like a complex concept, but it can help you understand yourself and your relationship with the universe through its various archetypes.

Chapter 3: Ma'at and the Tree of Life

Ma'at isn't just an ancient Egyptian goddess. She is also the foundational concept in Kemetic philosophy and the essence of the Tree of Life. Understanding Ma'at as a deity and a concept will help you learn more about ancient Egyptians, the principles they lived by, and how they are judged in the afterlife.

This chapter explores Ma'at as a divine law and a goddess, its role in balancing the universe, its influence on social norms, Ma'at's 42 principles, and a judgment scene from the ancient Egyptian afterlife.

Ma'at, the goddess behind the Kemetic philosophy.[a]

Exploring Ma'at

In ancient Egypt, deities weren't only creators or supernatural beings that brought thunder, rain, destruction, etc. They also represented concepts, values, and theories related to the cosmos and impacted every aspect of mankind's lives. Ancient Egyptians believed that ideology and religion were connected. Each god and goddess symbolizes principles that maintain balance in the universe and among individuals.

Ma'at is pronounced "may-et" and means "that which is straight," symbolizing harmony and order. She is the goddess of balance, harmony, justice, and truth. However, she is more than a deity. As a concept, Ma'at embodies divine law governing both the cosmos and human conduct.

According to ancient Egyptian cosmology, Ma'at principles laid the foundation of the country's civilization and provided laws to keep the universe in harmony and order. Individuals should follow these rules to establish structure spiritually, morally, socially, and in the cosmos.

Ancient Egyptians' religious beliefs involved more than praying to their deities and making offerings to appease them. They also performed rituals, followed a moral code, and made an effort to maintain harmony and make the world a better place as acts of worship. Aligning themselves with Ma'at's principles not only impacted their lives but also kept the universe from being in disarray.

Ra didn't create Ma'at just to be a goddess but as a divine law that governed mankind and other deities. Even though he was a supreme being and the king of the gods, Ra also upheld these principles and held them in high regard.

As a goddess, Ma'at is depicted as a woman with wings and a white ostrich feather on her head, symbolizing lightness, truth, and balance. The feather isn't an accessory. It played a major role in judging the dead in the afterlife. During the Weighing of the Heart rite, a person's heart is put on a scale and weighed against Ma'at's feather. The result determined whether the soul would be rewarded in the afterlife or punished. This ceremony reflects Ma'at's significance in ancient Egypt's cosmology.

Archaeologists and historians found much evidence to prove how Ma'at was highly revered. The plinth was one of her symbols. While it wasn't used to identify names, the plinth was usually seen under the thrones of gods and goddesses. Using it to signify Ma'at showed her influence on ancient Egyptian society. She also accompanied Ra on his daily journeys across the sky and protected him against Apophis in the underworld.

According to historian Margaret Bunson, Ma'at's role in the afterlife rituals evolved over the years into the concept of Ma'at and her principles, which drew a moral and ethical map that all Egyptians followed.

Ma'at was one of the oldest deities in ancient Egypt. She was Ra's daughter, was born at the beginning of creation, and was married to Thoth, the god of wisdom. It is believed that she was born when Ra created the universe. She used her powers to bring balance and order to the universe and ensured that all creation lived in harmony.

It is believed that Ma'at once ruled the Earth. However, mankind's evil ways caused her great sorrow, so she returned to the heavens. Ma'at was also responsible for regulating the stars and the seasons to maintain balance in heaven and Earth. She also made sure that the Nile flooding was beneficial and was used in agriculture instead of destroying crops and lands.

However, historians agree that Ma'at is more of a concept than a deity. Unlike Osiris, Isis, Set, and other gods and goddesses, she didn't have any myths associated with her or known personality traits. She wasn't a goddess that one related to or sympathized with, like other deities. She was merely an idea or set of principles that people abided by to live happily and morally.

Ma'at's Philosophy

- **Harmony (Maat):** It represents order and balance in the cosmos and communities.
- **Order (Maat):** Finding order within individuals and in their environments to maintain balance and stability.
- **Justice (Ma'at):** Enforcing justice among individuals and society, making sure that people treat each other and all the Divine's creatures fairly.
- **Propriety (Rit):** Teaching people to be respectful, appropriate, and dignified in every situation.
- **Balance (Mehen):** Everything should be in moderation, and people should avoid extremes to find harmony.

- **Reciprocity (Ife):** Understanding that all living creatures are connected on a deeper level.
- **Truth (Maakheru):** Making sure that one's thoughts, actions, and words are true. One should align oneself with cosmic truth.

Ma'at's Role in Maintaining the Equilibrium of the Universe

Ancient Egyptians believed that Ma'at was a unifying heavenly force that brought together nature and divine principles to create a universe built on order and harmony. She was responsible for seasonal changes, star movements, forces of nature, human behavior, and people's mental and emotional state.

Ma'at created a model for human behavior that was aligned with the will of all other deities. Her principles maintain order on Earth and in heaven. Ancient Egyptians believed that they would become part of the cosmos in the afterlife. As a result, they lived according to its divine laws (Ma'at's principles).

Ma'at represented the spirit of all living beings. Aligning oneself with her laws will help you find fulfillment and peace in this life and the next. However, if one doesn't follow her principles, they will have to face the consequences of their actions.

All forces of creation and destruction must be kept in balance. The ancient Egyptians believed in dualism and the necessity of having two opposing forces fighting against one another.

In the story of creation, after Ra created the universe, only chaos prevailed. He realized the need for order or chaos would destroy everything. Ra created Ma'at to bring harmony, structure, and balance the forces of destruction.

According to mythology, Ma'at's (harmony and order) opposing force is Isfet (chaos and disharmony). The pharaohs guarded Ma'at and upheld her principles because she protected them against Isfet, which could destroy the universe. Both had equal power, but they never used it to kill each other. They only fought.

The perfect example of this is the story of Ra, who followed Ma'at principles, and Apophis, who symbolized Isfet and chaos. While they fought every night, they never destroyed each other. The purpose of this story isn't defeating evil. It shows the significance of their daily battles to keep the universe in balance.

Ma'at's Influence on Governance, Laws, and Social Norms

Ma'at's principles influenced all aspects of ancient Egyptians' lives, including their governance and social norms. They brought stability and harmony to societies and the universe. Ma'at symbolized justice, order, and truth, which impacted laws, communities, and individuals.

Ma'at played an important role in creating societal roles and governance. Its principles guided people's actions and behavior. Each person should abide by her principles so that society and individuals can thrive.

The deities used Ma'at's scale to weigh Horus and Set's deeds.'

In the story of Osiris, Isis, and Set, Set represents chaos and goes against Ma'at's principles. He battled with Horus over the throne until the deities intervened and held an assembly similar to a court to decide who was the rightful ruler. The deities used Ma'at's scale to weigh Horus and Set's deeds.

Set wasn't a fair ruler as he didn't apply Ma'at's principles and brought chaos, injustice, and darkness to Egypt. Although Horus was young, impulsive, and less experienced, he believed in balance and order and wanted to be a just ruler like his father. As a result, the scale tipped in Horus's favor, and Ma'at declared him as the rightful king. In this version of the story, Set didn't die, allowing his chaos to balance with Horus's harmony.

Ancient Egyptians' laws were connected with their religion, and they regulated people's behaviors and actions. Since all citizens lived according to Ma'at's principles, they all had the same understanding of what justice, order, truth, and harmony meant. This brought communities together and created unity among societies.

The Responsibility of Pharaohs to Uphold Ma'at

The pharaohs were mediators between mankind and the deities. It was their duty to protect and uphold Ma'at's principles by creating laws that aligned with the goddess's teachings. A pharaoh was called "Lord of Ma'at" and played the biggest role in keeping the universe balanced.

Kings were judged on whether they could maintain stability, peace, and prosperity in their kingdoms. The pharaohs were seen as the personification of Ma'at and should apply laws that enforce justice in society.

Before making any decision, kings sought Ma'at's wisdom and her principles. All their laws should align with her divine truth. However, pharaohs must also adhere to these principles in their personal life and daily interactions. This shows that every person in ancient Egyptian societies must follow Ma'at, no matter their position or status.

Ancient Egyptian queen Hatshepsut ruled over the country during a time when mainly males were allowed to rule. However, she didn't use her royal lineage to become queen. She embodied Ma'at's principles, which brought prosperity to the lands and allowed people to live in peace and stability.

The 42 Principles of Ma'at

The 42 principles of Ma'at, also called "The Declaration of Innocence" or "Negative Confessions," are principles that ancient Egyptians followed throughout their lives. They acted as a moral and ethical guide to teach people proper conduct. In the afterlife, the dead recited them during the Weighing of the Heart ceremony.

Below are the 42 principles with greetings to judges (deities) and their regions, some of which exist in the afterlife.

1. Hail, Usekh-nemmt, who comest forth from Anu, I have not sinned.
2. Hail, Hept-khet, who comest forth from Kher-aha, I have not committed robbery or violence.

3. Hail, Fenti, who comest forth from Khemenu, I have not stolen.
4. Hail, Am-khaibit, who comes forth from Qnet, I have not slain men and women.
5. Hail, Neha-her, who comest forth from Rasta, I have not stolen grain.
6. Hail, Ruruti, who comest forth from Heaven, I have not purloined offerings.
7. Hail, Arfi-em-khet, who comest forth from Suat, I have not stolen the property of God.
8. Hail, Neba, who comes and goes, I have not uttered lies.
9. Hail, Set-qesu, who comest forth from Hensu, I have not carried away food.
10. Hail, Utu-nesert, who comest forth from Het-ka-Ptah, I have not uttered curses.
11. Hail, Qerrti, who comest forth from Amentet, I have not committed adultery.
12. Hail, Hraf-haf, who comest forth from thy cavern, I have made none to weep.
13. Hail, Basti, who comest forth from Bast, I have not eaten the heart.
14. Hail, Ta-retiu, who comest forth from the night, I have not attacked any man.
15. Hail, Unem-snef, who comest forth from the execution chamber, I am not a man of deceit.
16. Hail, Unem-besek, who comest forth from Mabit, I have not stolen cultivated land.
17. Hail, Neb-Maat, who comest forth from Maati, I have not been an eavesdropper.
18. Hail, Tenemiu, who comest forth from Bast, I have not slandered anyone.
19. Hail, Sertiu, who comest forth from Anu, I have not been angry without just cause.
20. Hail, Tutu, who comest forth from Ati, I have not debauched the wife of any man.

21. Hail, Uamenti, who comest forth from the Khebt chamber, I have not debauched the wives of other men.
22. Hail, Maa-antuf, who comest forth from Per-Menu, I have not polluted myself.
23. Hail, Her-uru, who comest forth from Nehatu, I have terrorized none.
24. Hail, Khemiu, who comes forth from Kaui, I have not transgressed the law.
25. Hail, Shet-kheru, who comest forth from Urit, I have not been angry.
26. Hail, Nekhenu, who comes forth from Heat, I have not shut my ears to the words of truth.
27. Hail, Kenemti, who comest forth from Kenmet, I have not blasphemed.
28. Hail, An-hetep-f, who comest forth from Sau, I am not a man of violence.
29. Hail, Sera-kheru, who comest forth from Unaset, I have not been a stirrer up of strife.
30. Hail, Neb-heru, who comest forth from Netchfet, I have not acted with undue haste.
31. Hail, Sekhriu, who comest forth from Uten, I have not pried into others' matters.
32. Hail, Neb-abui, who comest forth from Sauti, I have not multiplied my words in speaking.
33. Hail, Nefer-Tem, who comest forth from Het-ka-Ptah, I have wronged none, I have done no evil.
34. Hail, Tem-Sepu, who comest forth from Tetu, I have not worked witchcraft against the king.
35. Hail, Ari-em-ab-f, who comest forth from Tebu, I have never stopped the flow of water from my neighbor.
36. Hail, Ahi, who comest forth from Nu, I have never raised my voice.
37. Hail, Uatch-rekhit, who comest forth from Sau, I have not cursed God.
38. Hail, Neheb-ka, who comest forth from thy cavern, I have not acted with arrogance.

39. Hail, Neheb-nefert, who comest forth from thy cavern, I have not stolen the bread of the gods.

40. Hail, Tcheser-tep, who comest forth from the shrine, I have not carried away the khenfu cakes from the spirits of the dead.

41. Hail, An-af, who comest forth from Maati, I have not snatched away the bread of the child, nor treated with contempt the god of my city.

42. Hail, Hetch-abhu, who comest forth from Ta-she, I have not slain the cattle belonging to the god.

Judgment Scene from the Book of the Dead

Ancient Egyptians called their afterlife "A'Aru," meaning "The Field of Reeds," a heavenly place where people spend eternity. However, not everyone was destined to spend the afterlife in paradise. They first stood before judges and had their hearts weighed on a scale against Ma'at's feather to determine if they did enough good deeds that warranted them a place in heaven. This part provides a scene from the Book of the Dead of Hunefer.

Hunefer was a scribe to Pharaoh Seti I during the 19th dynasty, and this was his judgment. Hunefer kneeled before the 14 judges of deities: Ra, Atum, Shu, Tefnut, Geb, Nut, Horus, Isis, Nephthys, Hu, and Sia, and the personifications of the Western, Northern, and Southern Roads.

He held hands with Anubis, the god of embalming and protector of the dead. Anubis is depicted as a man with a jackal's head. He took Hunefer to Ma'at's scale, where the Weighing of the Heart Ceremony took place to determine whether he deserved to go to the Field of Reeds or not.

Ma'at's feather was on the right side of the scale, weighing against Hunter's heart, which was on the left side. The ancient Egyptians chose to weigh the heart since they believed it was home to one's character, intellect, and emotions and would show if a person led an honest or dishonest life.

Ammit, a female demon, sat below the scale. She had the face of a crocodile, its head and half of its body looked like a lion, and the other half resembled a hippopotamus. If a person's heart weighed more than Ma'at's feather, they

Ma'at's feather.[10]

were bad individuals who led a sinful life and didn't deserve the afterlife. Ammit would then devour their heart, and the person would cease to exist.

Thoth, the god of spells, scribes, and writing, stood watching the scale to record the results. Unlike Ammt, who stood eagerly waiting to devour the heart, Thoth didn't show any emotion.

Luckily for Hunefer, his heart was lighter than Ma'at's feather, and he could spend eternity in the afterlife. Hunefer was happy and relieved. He passed the hardest test of his life.

Horus stood on Hunefer's right. After the results, he pointed his right hand to his father, Osiris, who was sitting among the other deity judges. Horus took Hunefer to meet his father and the other gods.

Ancient Egyptians believed in free will and that every person made their own decisions and should suffer the consequences of their actions. If they lived according to Ma'at's principles, they would go to the Field of Reeds and reunite with their loved ones who passed before them.

Following Ma'at's principles indicates that you lived a good life. You were honest, kind, and treated people with love and respect. You didn't steal or commit sins and upheld truth and justice. This brought balance to the ancient Egyptians' hearts and secured their place in the afterlife.

Incorporating Maat into Modern Life

Live by Ma'at's principles and incorporate them into your daily life.

Ethical Decision-Making

Make decisions according to your ethics and morals. Don't make ones that go against your beliefs just to make money or advance in your career. Ask yourself each time if it will harm someone. For instance, if your decision concerns your job, make sure it doesn't affect your team, ruin someone's reputation, or cause your company any financial loss.

You should also collect all the facts and relevant information before you make a decision. Do your research, ask other people, and find out what the outcome will be? If you or someone else will get harmed, consider other options that won't harm you or others. You should strive to achieve justice, truth, and harmony by making fair decisions without compromising your values, dignity, or others' feelings. Implement your decision, but consider the outcome. Remember that you can always go back to change it if you aren't comfortable with it.

Fostering Harmony in Relationships

Creating harmony in your relationships will keep you and your loved ones happy and prevent conflicts and fights.

- **Communication:** Express your feelings and needs openly and clearly to your partner, friends, family, etc. If you are upset, speak up and tell them how you feel. Don't keep them guessing or act passive-aggressive. Listen to them when they share something with you. Don't interrupt; just give your opinion. Listen to understand, not to respond. Create a safe space for your loved ones to come to you with their problems without feeling judged or attacked.

- **Respect:** You should respect your loved one's feelings, thoughts, opinions, time, decisions, and individuality. Accept that you have different beliefs, and don't try to reinforce yours on them. Respect their boundaries, and don't push your limits or pressure them when they feel uncomfortable. You should also protect your boundaries and be firm if someone crosses them.

- **Flexibility:** Plans, circumstances, and situations can change. Instead of fighting them, you need to adapt and make adjustments when necessary. Unexpected events may occur, so you need to navigate these challenges with your loved ones to maintain stability and peace.

- **Empathy:** It is the ability to put yourself in someone's shoes and understand their thoughts, feelings, and experiences as if they were your own. Empathy will help you connect with your loved ones on a deeper level and make them feel heard, seen, and understood.

Be Honest in All Your Interactions

Embody Ma'at's truthfulness and remain honest in all your interactions. Don't lie to make yourself feel good or to get out of a bad situation. Lying always leads to serious consequences. When you tell the truth, people will trust and respect you, and you will create strong relationships.

Always Be Fair

Like Ma'at, you should always choose balance and justice. Be fair during conflicts or disputes. Don't make false accusations or put someone down to gain the upper hand. Find solutions that will satisfy all parties instead of only looking out for yourself.

Maintain Order and Harmony

Talk about your problems with your loved ones instead of arguing and disrupting your relationships. Be straightforward and clear during conversations. People aren't mind-readers, so don't leave them guessing. Set clear boundaries and rules on which behaviors you don't tolerate to maintain order in your interactions.

Justice and Moral Integrity

In both your personal and professional life, be a good person and don't give in to temptation. Stand up for what you believe in, even if you are alone.

Practical Exercises

Ma'at Daily Reflection

Reflect on your daily actions and decisions through the lens of Ma'at. At the end of the day, write down one action that upheld truth, balance, or harmony and one that could have been more aligned with these principles. Set an intention for the next day to act in greater accordance with Ma'at, fostering continuous self-improvement.

_____

_____

_____

Feather of Ma'at Visualization

Sit quietly and visualize your heart being weighed against the feather of Ma'at. Picture the feather representing truth and balance. Do you feel any emotional weight (e.g., guilt, anger, or dishonesty) tipping the scale? Release that weight through deep breathing. Take a long, deep breath through your mouth and imagine you are inhaling harmony, truth, and light. Exhale and imagine the air you release is the emotional weight. You can also use an affirmation, such as, "I let go of what disrupts harmony and embrace the lightness of Ma'at."

Even though Ma'at's principles were created thousands of years ago, they are still relevant today. Morals don't change over time. These principles are key to living a happy and peaceful life. If each person upholds these laws in their daily interactions, the whole society will change for the better. Embody Ma'at in every aspect of your life, and you will feel fulfilled in this world and the next.

Chapter 4: Tree of Life Numerology

This chapter examines the role of numerology in Kemetic spirituality and the Tree of Life. It reveals how numbers were not only tools for measurement but also symbols of divine principles. You will learn the sacred meanings behind them and how to unlock deeper insights into the function of the Kemetic Tree of Life and its spheres.

Numerology has a role to play in Kemetic spirituality. [11]

The Role of Numerology in Kemetic Culture and How it Connects to the Tree of Life

Numerology fits into Kemetic Culture and aligns with the Tree of Life as it links to principles of nature and divine forces, revealing the workings of the underworld, heavens, and earth. They also symbolize Neteru and the aspect of creation they represent. Each number connects to a cosmic principle, revealing the powers, qualities, and stages of spiritual enlightenment. They also help you read the map of the Tree of Life and spiritual ascent and growth.

For instance, number one refers to Atum and the origins of life and the universe. Number three represents Osiris and the cycle of life, death, and resurrection. The god of knowledge and wisdom, Thoth, represents the number seven, the understanding and awakening of the spirit. These numbers represent all phases of spiritual growth, with the Tree of Life carving out the path of spiritual ascent to the divine realm. Leaving the physical world behind to enter higher dimensions requires the tree's spheres. These spheres, or sefirot, are assigned numbers to reflect one's evolution.

Number one reflects Keter, the first sphere, and is your starting point where you unite with Neteru. Number four, the fourth sphere named Chesed, is where you'll open up to the other world. It requires your kindness and compassion. Malkuth is the sphere assigned to number ten, the phase of divine manifestation on Earth. It signals that your journey is complete.

Balance of the physical and spiritual world is maintained through the Tree of Life's numerology. You have the sixth sphere, Tiferet, associated with the number six, representing the beauty of the balance of opposites, like the one between the realms. Another example of Kemetic culture's mysticism and mythology is reflected in the Tree of Life's third sphere. The number three signifies the cyclical nature of life, the sun, seasons, and the soul's journey.

Numbers are Universal Symbols that Represent Energies, Patterns, and Divine Laws

Numbers have communicated some of the most powerful meanings of the universe. These universal symbols represent energies, patterns, and cosmic laws with directness and clarity. Numbers resonate with different aspects of life, as seen in sacred geometry and the Neteru system of the Kemetic Tree of Life.

Each number has a vibrational frequency that connects to the qualities and forces of nature. For instance, number one represents the beginning of everything. Dynamic forces and patterns in nature can be observed through the order of one's cells, the path of the soul's journey, and the universe. You'll notice the number four is a recurring pattern of stability and structure, such as the four elements of air, earth, fire, and water, the four seasons, the four cardinal directions, and the four states of matter, gas, liquid, plasma, and solid.

Numbers decipher divine laws and universal principles, such as the number two representing duality and the concept of opposites. Everything has a counterpart, from light and dark to male and female and good and bad. They also depict the flow of life through the phases of nature's cycles and evolution. The ending stages of human development can be found in the number nine, resonating with the finality of transformation and how it leads to an opportunity to start a new path.

The Importance of Numbers 1, 3, and 7

Numbers like one, three, and seven are vital in Kemetic spirituality, beliefs, and numerology. These numbers dissect the forces of universal law and can deepen your understanding of growth, transformation, and creativity patterns.

- **Number 1**

One is associated with Atum, also known as Ra, the creator god who embodies oneness. It is depicted as the center point of creation from where life originally emerged and all energy and patterns flow. Number one reflects the idea that all life, energy, and matter originate from Atum's creation of the world. The first sphere of the Tree of Life, Keter, symbolizes the connection to the divine source.

- **Number 3**

Three represents the balance of these fundamental principles: creation and preservation. It reflects a force that governs the natural world: the manifestation of ideas. Preservation refers to the maintenance of creation, promoting harmony and structure in the world. Destruction is the necessary and inevitable ending or transformation of living things to make way for new life. The third sphere, Binah, reflects the cyclical nature of existence as presented by the Tree of Life. Osiris, the god of the afterlife, keeps the consistent flow of life, death, and rebirth.

- **Number 7**

Seven is linked to Thoth, the god of wisdom, and represents spiritual cycles, completion, and perfection. It reflects the fulfillment and completion of the growth process, like the seven cardinal virtues of Ma'at, to achieve perfection in humanity: balance, order, justice, truth, reciprocity, compassion, and harmony. In Kemetic myth, Thoth is tied to the seven stages of development, corresponding to the seven cycles of the soul's journey. The Tree of Life's seventh sphere, Netzach, conveys similar principles: endurance, evolution, and spiritual triumph over material challenges.

How Numbers Symbolize Divine Principles and the Cosmic Order

There is a correlation between specific Neteru (deities) and numbers in Kemetic spirituality. These numbers interpret different aspects of nature, creation, and the universe, combining myth and numerology to discover their cosmic roles in nature.

The Number 1

One is linked to Atum (Ra) - this god symbolizes the source of creation and how everything is born of one single point in the abyss. The number and deity emphasize the importance of unity over division and symbolize wholeness.

The Number 2

Two is associated with Isis. She represents motherly love, nurture, magic, and duality as the feminine principle complements masculine energy. Both signify the power of divine pairings and healing.

The Number 3

Three aligns with Osiris, the god of rebirth, and the afterlife governs the divine order, transformation, and resurrection because it symbolizes the cycle of nature: life, death, and renewal.

The Number 4

Four is associated with the goddess Ma'at, who symbolizes the foundation and the structure of four, such as the four directions and seasons. Four upholds universal law and nature's principles just as Ma'at spread order to the four corners of the world.

The Number 5

Five is linked to Horus, the scribe of protection and power. The Neter and number in Kemetic myth signal virtues such as action, kingship, and divine rule. Divine perception, awareness, and vision are emblematic of Horus' powers, correlating to the five senses.

The Number 6

Six is ruled by Hathor, who symbolizes connection and happiness. This number resonates with balance in relationships, a symbol of love, beauty, peace, and joy. Six elements were used to honor Hathor, such as music, dance, food, and wine, since she conveyed the art of pleasure, intoxication, and celebration.

The Number 7

Seven is governed by Thoth, the god of magic and wisdom who brings spiritual truth. Seven means one is approaching sacred order, knowledge, power, and divine awakening. Divine knowledge was attributed to those who succeeded and were thus granted the judgment of Thoth, who had observed their souls' progress.

The Number 8

Eight is connected to the Ogdoad of Hermopolis, representing the strength and authority of the eight primeval Neteru. Together, they symbolize elements of creation, such as water and darkness, and the cosmic balance. Just like the number, the Ogdoad of Hermopolis is a symbol of infinity, reflecting the regeneration found in mythic cycles.

The Number 9

Nine is ruled by the Ennead of Heliopolis. The group of nine Neteru follows the sun god Ra. The number nine is associated with the totality and completion of universal order and the peak of cosmic cycles before starting over. Members of the Ennead represent the continuation of divine energy and family, symbolic of the organized structure and lineage of Neteru.

The Structure and Function of the Kemetic Tree of Life and Its Spheres

The 10 spheres of the Tree of Life embody numerical principles that reflect the steps of spiritual ascent, from material grounding to divine unity. The structure and function of the sefirot are associated with numbers to represent the stage of consciousness one is at.

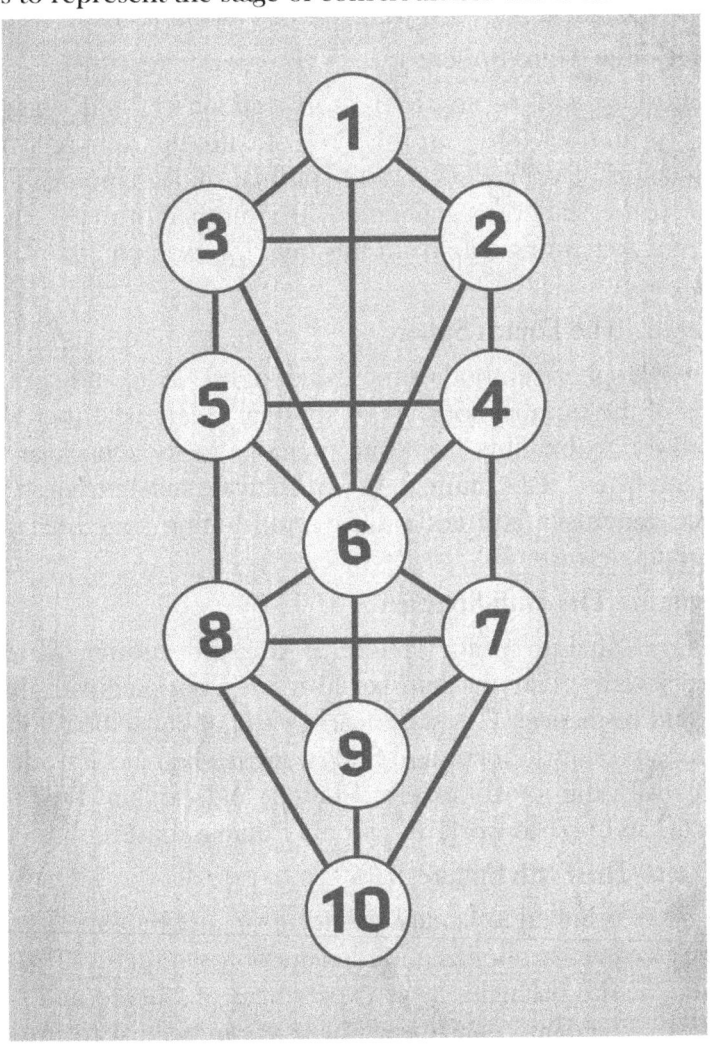

1. Keter - The First Sphere

The first sphere, the crown, embodies the numerical principle of number one, which is unity. It represents the mystical starting point of one's spiritual journey. It's where a spiritual spark or force of energy ignites your growth.

2. Chochmah - The Second Sphere

The second sphere is linked to the principles of number two: intuition and spiritual thought. At the top-right pillar is the birth of the seed of wisdom that comes to life and the beginning of polarity, representing the father principle in creation. It plants knowledge and growth, the second step toward your spiritual ascent in the Tree of Life.

3. Binah - The Third Sphere

The third sphere relates to reason, rationality, and analysis, the principles of number three. In the Tree of Life, this sphere symbolizes the culmination of your wisdom and spiritual understanding. The third point marks the start of a generation, the mother principle in nature. Spheres four to ten originate from this one, for example, the seven days of creation.

4. Chesed - The Fourth Sphere

The fourth sphere embodies mercy, kindness, love, and compassion, the motifs of the number four. Your spiritual ascent is at the expansion stage, and you're building a cosmic memory to look back at how far you've come from the beginning. As you cultivate self-awareness, you will experience generosity and goodwill, demonstrating your might, power, action, and tenderness.

5. Gevurah - The Fifth Sphere

The Tree of Life's fifth sphere is the fifth power of god and represents severity. Like the number five, it is associated with discipline, strength, and resilience. This stage teaches you about setting boundaries, self-control, and how to focus and find strength when tackling challenges. It balances with the fourth sphere, Chesed, and explains how universal law operates and how to work with it rather than against it.

6. Tiferet - The Sixth Sphere

The sphere is linked to beauty, cosmic love, and the divine sun. It sits at the tree's center, symbolizing the beauty of a symmetrical balance. At this phase, you are balancing your experiences of Chesed and Gevurah, the practice of mediation and peace between archetypal realms and the human world to combine strength and love and bring a sense of unity into existence.

7. Netzach - The Seventh Sphere

The seventh sphere, called victory, is a representation of completeness and eternity in the Tree of Life. It symbolizes mastery, from your endurance and perseverance to victory over your baser instincts. Like the number seven, this sphere is about determination and overcoming obstacles and emotions.

8. Hod - The Eighth Sphere

The eighth sphere is tied to glory, acknowledgment, and humility. Like the number eight, this sphere signifies infinity and one's vibrational frequency, intellect, magnificence, the power of a humble heart, and appreciation of divine creation.

9. Yesod - The Ninth Sphere

Number nine refers to the foundation of reality and omnipotence. As you spiritually ascend in the Tree of Life, this sphere represents the stage of grounding yourself, keeping in touch with reality in the physical realm, while reaching higher dimensions of consciousness in the astral and heavenly realms.

10. Malkuth - The Tenth Sphere

The number ten is linked to finality and completion. In the Tree of Life, this phase symbolizes the outward manifestation of divine energy, such as the four elements. The tenth sphere is referred to as a kingdom, such as the kingdom of heaven, indicating that the journey is complete. In mythology, one is ready to begin the next phase on a higher, more evolved level, also known as the return to god.

How Sacred Geometry Reflects Numerological Principles and Aligns with the Tree of Life's Spheres

The ten spheres are connected through twenty-two paths, with the first sphere at the top and the tenth sphere at the bottom. The shapes (triangles, pyramids, etc.) of sacred geometry align with the same mythic motifs of the Neteru system.

- **The Circle - Number 0 - 1**

The circle symbolizes the number zero or one in sacred geometry. All shapes are derived from the circle, making it the building block of geometry. It is emblematic of eternity and wholeness, reflecting that a circle shape is an endless cycle that repeats itself. In the Tree of Life, this number represents the first sphere, the crown or Keter, as it is the source from which all energy flows. The numerological principle and the first sphere in the Kemetic system relate to the ultimate connection, spirit, truth, and essence of the divine Neteru.

- **Two Intersecting Circles - Number 2**

The geometric shape of number two is called Vesica Piscis and can be tricky because it sometimes looks like two intersecting circles, with the overlap depicting an oval shape. Other times, it is two symmetrical circles stacked on top of each other or beside each other with a vertical line drawn in between.

The second sphere and the geometric shape symbolize what is at the heart of creation, duality, separation, and polarity, as Chochmah exists by separating from the unity of the first sphere while remaining bonded. When the Vesica Piscis is depicted as a line, it creates the illusion of division and paradox, but this shows an everlasting connection between two opposite forces. This geometric shape embodies expansion and consciousness as it proves that two opposites can always reunite and synergize. In myth, the number two has always represented duality and the importance of two sides to make a whole, such as yin and yang.

- **The Triangle - Number 3**

The triangle in sacred geometry reflects the number of creation: three, the foundation of Kemetic culture. This number symbolizes growth, the triad or divine pyramid, representing the father, mother, and child. The Tree of Life emphasizes this cycle of creation, preservation, and destruction with its third sphere, Binah, epitomizing structure and understanding.

In sacred geometry, the triangle represents trinities and how they create balance, strength, and stability. It is often depicted as a conclusive result, such as the rule of three, meaning the emitting of negative or positive energy returns threefold, like karmic justice.

- **The Square - Number 4**

The square or cube represents the three-dimensionality of space and the natural cycles of physical matter. It solidifies the foundational structure of balance and stability and is associated with numerical principle four, the foundation of the physical realm's structure.

The square reflects the solidity and permanence of the physical world. The Kemetic Tree's system showcases the principles of the number four, with the goddess Ma'at symbolizing justice and truth, creating harmony and balance in the universal order. The fourth sphere, Chesed, is necessary to develop relationships and personal qualities.

- **The Pentagram/Pentagon - Number 5**

The five sides of the Pentagon or the five-pointed star signify protection, life, and love. The number five is considered the key to life and interweaves all elements of life in a sacred marriage. It infuses a spirit, essence, or consciousness into the world to blind all life and matter, making the geometric shape of the number five the quintessence of the perfect divinity and synergy. Consider the five senses, hearing, sight, smell, touch, and taste, and how they all work together.

The number five in sacred geometry and the fifth sphere in the Neteru system reflects principles, such as personal change, power, and freedom. Horus, the god of kingship, was associated with discipline and strength due to his protective nature, defending against negativity.

- **The Hexagon - Number 6**

The hexagon represents the organic equilibrium and perfect symmetry of creation, including all its components and contradictions. It reflects the principles of the number six: love, harmony, and balance. It creates a kinship between the material and spiritual aspects of living and an inner peace between humans' minds and hearts.

The number six also signifies the law of correspondence, the centeredness that mirrors all patterns and ensures their repetition. The Tree of Life's sixth sphere, Tiferet, symbolizes the beauty and integration of opposites, bringing everything together, just as the goddess of love and music, Hathor, reflected how love stabilizes the universe.

- **The Heptagon - Number 7**

The heptagon is considered the hidden center of the hexagon. This shape symbolizes the number seven and the concept of mysticism and spiritual growth because seven has always been the number of mystical power. It signifies the spirit ruling over physical forms and expresses the rhythm of life through complete cycles, such as the seven days of the week, seven colors of the rainbow, and seven musical notes.

Number seven reflects the end stage of a cycle and connects to the Tree of Life's seventh sphere, Netzach, which is associated with endurance, victory, and perfection. In the Neteru system, this is reflective of Thoth, the god of wisdom, aligning with the motifs of seven, purity, unconditional love, and intellectual growth to achieve higher awareness.

- **The Octagon - Number 8**

Depicted in the shape of the octagon are power, infinity, and eternity. The number eight symbolizes the stability and infinite magic of physical reality. The eternal cycle of abundance and strength is reflected in the number eight. You can see this expressed through the transformation and resurrection after a cycle. Eight, following seven – the completion of a cycle – signifies the boomerang effect of karmic law. In myth, this can be seen through the Ogdoad.

In Kemetic culture, the goddess Sekhmet represented the principles of eight, the power of regeneration, transformation, and balance in the material and spiritual realm. Hod, the eighth sphere in the Tree of Life, also aligns with the potential for growth, understanding, glory, and humility to appreciate the abundance and strength of divine order.

- **The Nonagon - Number 9**

In sacred geometry, the number nine represents the nonagon. The number resonates with the psychological teachings of the nine-pointed figure called the Enneagram. This shape and number houses the three worlds, also known as the triple trinity or the triple triad in geometry, the synthesis of the source, the universe, and the human being.

The numerological principles of number nine are closely tied to the ninth sphere in the Tree of Life as both are a symbol of mastery, compassion, and completion, reflecting the end stage that leads to abundance, prosperity, and even magical power – think of the gestation period lasting 9 months. Nine symbolizes the longevity of a cycle and the return to unity or oneness. In Kemetic mythology, the ninth sphere leads one to a greater cycle composed of regeneration, truth, eternal love, and achievement.

Practical Exercises:

Numerical Meditation with the Tree of Life

1. Choose a quiet area without distractions. You can hang a drawing of the Tree of Life to help you focus on the sphere of your choice.
2. Close your eyes, inhale through your nose, and release the breath through your mouth. Feel your body relaxing into the ideal state of consciousness.
3. Visualize your body becoming grounded through roots that connect you to the number and sphere of your choice. The Tree of Life's sphere is a bright light shining over you.
4. Focus on your number and its principles. Imagine them becoming engraved in your mind like energy infusing your spirit.
5. Feel the concepts of each number manifesting inside you. For example, if you meditate on number 3, the principles of the third sphere, such as transformation and preservation, will flow through you. If your number is 10, then the concepts of completion and manifestation will radiate from the 10th sphere into you.
6. Reflect on their wisdom by acknowledging what these concepts mean to you and how you can apply them to your spiritual journey. Is this meditation practice encouraging you to create as the third sphere might? Or is the number 10 informing you to transform aspects of your life?
7. End the exercise with gratitude for the Tree of Life's wisdom.

Creating a Numerological Map

1. Calculate your life path and expression number. Your life path number is found by adding up the digits of your date of birth until you get a single-digit number. Your expression number is formed by assigning the letter of your full name to a letter of the alphabet. The alphabet follows numerical order (from 1 to 9). For example: A-1, B-2, etc. Reduce your final number to a single digit.
2. These key numbers will reveal the purpose of your journey and the challenges to prepare for - and will guide you in the right direction. For example, if you've chosen number 1 as a life path

number, you will probably be guided on a tour of introspection and independence.
3. Reflect on what the numerical spheres on the Tree of Life, corresponding with your life path and expression numbers, have to say. For instance, assuming your life path number is 1, it may be influencing your need for leadership and encouraging you to take charge.
4. Your intuition will kick in as you write down questions to map out your numerological path. These questions should include asking how the energies of your numbers affect your current situation and how you can interact with them and fulfill your spiritual needs.

Personal Numerology and the Spheres
1. Calculate your personal number using either your name or date of birth.
2. Align your number with the Tree of Life spheres. For example, number 9, Yesod, stands for foundation and emotional stability.
3. Apply what your number's sphere represents to your personal life. For instance, number 9 might suggest you improve your emotional health to set a strong foundation for spiritual growth.
4. Integrate your number's energy in your spiritual practice:
    - Meditate on your number and sphere by visualizing its qualities and principles.
    - Reflect on its teachings and how it can influence this stage of your life.
    - Focus on ways to adopt these traits in your personal life.

Chapter 5: Ascending the Kemetic Tree of Life

Besides the numerical aspect of ascent you've learned about in the previous chapter, a journey through the Kemetic Tree of Life also has the purpose of spiritual progression toward higher consciousness and unity with the divine. This chapter discusses how this path of ascent works, detailing what it truly means to ascend through the Tree of Life. Reading it, you'll learn about the stages of the journey, what challenges you may face in each, and the principles that lead individuals toward higher enlightenment on their travels across the Tree. At the end of the chapter, you'll find a meditative exercise for ascending the Kemetic Tree of Life.

The Kemetic Tree of Life also has the purpose of spiritual progression toward higher consciousness.[12]

The Tree of Life as a Symbol of Spiritual Progression

The Kemetic Tree of Life is a powerful symbol of spiritual ascension, emphasizing the strength it takes to complete the journey toward enlightenment, as well as the growth and transformation individuals experience after each passing stage. Trees in nature have always been seen as symbols of strength, and this isn't different from the Tree of Life either. Just like trees in nature can survive the toughest of challenges and grow their crown and roots, the Tree of Life takes you on a journey that teaches you that you persevere and grow if you work toward enlightenment.

The Tree of Life is also the symbol of stability. It consists of three pillars: one associated with masculinity, one with femininity, and one with feminine energy. While the masculine energy provides the force and challenges to expand your spiritual wisdom, the feminine is more passive and is characterized by the compaction of spiritual wisdom you've gathered. The middle pillar offers balance, tying the other two and providing them (and the entire Tree) the equilibrium necessary to persevere through the challenges of the journey.

As trees grow slowly and steadily, it stands to reason that the Tree of Life would be an excellent symbol of growth and progression. Moreover, trees are always in a cycle of growth - they go through one every year. In the same vein, ascension through the Tree of Life takes you across several cycles of growth. During each of these cycles, you absorb knowledge, which allows you to continue growing. At the end of a cycle, trees change, and so does an individual who reaches the end of a stage through the ascension journey. Yet, just like the changes trees experience across the seasons and years, each cycle through the ascension brings you opportunities to grow and become stronger and more resilient. They bring challenges, and facing these helps gather more knowledge. What you learn helps you adapt during the next phase, where you face other opportunities and challenges. This continues until you reach the root of the Tree, where enlightenment and unification with the divine await.

Yes, unlike trees in nature, ascension through the Kemetic Tree of Life is from the crown to the roots. The ultimate goal is living in alignment with the principle of Ma'at, and this is only possible if you learn to adhere to the principles by traversing through the stages of the

Tree of Life, beginning from the top. As you cross each stage, you'll encounter spheres, which represent the stages embodying qualities and wisdom you need to gather to reach enlightenment. Each sphere will help you understand the divine more, making it easier to unite with its energy.

The Stages of the Tree of Life

As you would imagine, ascending the Tree of Life is quite a transformational journey. You go through several spheres, which are also called sephirot. These are the stages that bring higher awareness of why everything manifests in your life and how you can manifest everything you want to see, experience, or connect with. In other words, each sefirot represents a spiritual quality or virtue to master, and after you harness all of them, you become more aware of everything and everyone around you, including the divine and its manifestations.

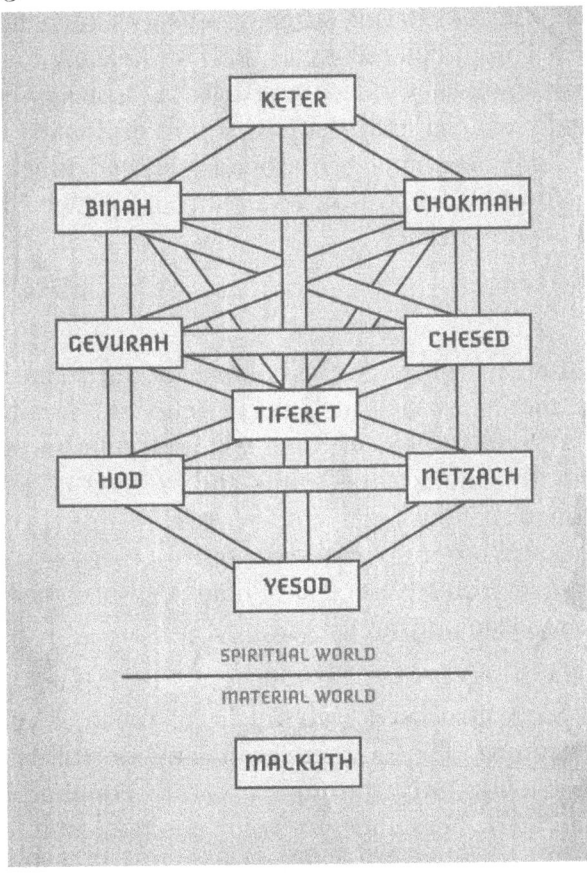

The sefirot are allocated across three triads: the intellectual, the emotional, and the instinctual. The intellectual triad includes Chokmah, Binah, and Da'at; the emotional one encompasses Chesed, Gevurah, and Tiferet, while the intellectual triad encircles the Netzach, Yod, and Yesod. However, before Chokmah in the first triad comes the crown or Keter, and after Yesod comes the divine kingdom or Malkuth.

Keter

Located at the top of the Tree of Life, Keter, the Crown of the Tree of Life, moves energy across all directions – human energy from bottom to top and the divine one from top to bottom. Keter establishes a link between divine wisdom and the human world and its energies. This leads to a higher awareness, from what's just beyond regular human consciousness to everything above and beyond everyone and everything in the universe. People start out with the knowledge they gather in the human world, but they can become aware of wisdom beyond it. For example, when you start having stronger sensory experiences, this may be the sign that you've entered Keter and are heading toward the first triad, Chokmah. You may notice you have a stronger sense of taste, touch, or smell, or you may have a more profound awareness of situations that have been going on around you (and which you haven't understood before). What you discover through Keter will affect and shape the rest of your journey.

Intellectual Triad

Chokmah

Emerging straight from Keter, Chokmah is the sefirah of wisdom. Here is where the energy that fuels deeper curiosity is born. It's where the thought you've uncovered in Keter will arise fully and give way to a mental capacity to embrace the truths and abstract concepts you are about to encounter. Noticing a sudden urge to dive deeply into the nature of reality and use more creative thought processes while doing so may indicate that you're crossing Chokmah. It's the sefirah that encourages you to lean on your gut feelings.

Binah

Another sefirah associated with intellect, Binah, stands for even deeper understanding. This is where your intuition will become a true and conscious guiding force, prompting you to continue reflecting on everything you learn. Listening to your intuition will force you to contemplate truths you haven't even considered before. Binah is where the awareness and knowledge you've gathered so far translate into specific ideas. As you learn to embrace the different perspectives, your ideas solidify, and you get a structure of a plan/goal you can set for your growth.

Binah and Chokmah are considered the originators of the rest of the sefirot, which isn't a coincidence. Together, they provide a seed for an idea, then bring out its potential, allowing you to proceed and grow, just like they allow the Tree of Life to prosper and thrive by conceiving the other, lower sefirot. Besides being a powerful intellectual kickstarter, Binah and Chokmah are also a magnificent combination of energy. From this combination, forces to use the energy (and the awareness and knowledge you gain) are born. Chokmah and Binah also give each other direction, allowing seekers to navigate the ascension through the Tree of Life right from the start.

Da'at

The third intellectual sefirah, Da'at, may be confusing to some. It represents the knowing, yet it is like a blank page. Do you know why? Because it's a page where you can record your reflection on the knowledge you gathered in Chokmah and the potential revealed to you in Binah. When you're ready to expand your thoughts beyond what you've learned so far, it's a clear sign that you've reached Da'at. It encourages you to fully integrate the gathered wisdom, form new ideas, and even reflect on conflicting truths. The goal is to find the balance between the different ideas you feel inspired to pursue and become able to set aside elements of thoughts that don't play a role in finalizing your ideas.

Emotional Triad

Chesed

Associated with love, Chesed encourages deep affection toward the ideas and goals you've formed and set to pursue. It fosters kindness, compassion, and mercy. The resurgence of these emotions may indicate an individual's arrival at Chesed. All that intellectual energy you gather across the first triad would only lead to the relentless pursuit of new ideas, which, while beneficial for encouraging creativity, can also lead to burnout - emotional, mental, physical, and spiritual. It can hinder your journey of ascension toward enlightenment. Tempering your rising intellectual energy with an emotional one, Chesed will help you prevent this from happening. It helps you see the emotional side of things, heal, and navigate your journey without losing yourself in the process. It can even help you bring back emotions you've repressed and deal with them with love and compassion. Feeling ready to do this could also be a sign that you're in Chesed.

Gevurah

Sometimes considered the sister of Chesed, Gevurah is the second emotional sefirah. However, unlike her brother, Gevurah fosters a more cautious approach. This sefirah is also referred to as strength or boundaries, as it highlights the need for placing limits and restoring balance between right and wrong. You see, not every emotion you experience and learn to express in Chesed will be the right one, nor could anyone be expected to deal with all the emotions they encounter. This is where crossing in Gevurah will come in handy. It encourages you to set boundaries for the energies and emotions you want to deal with and grow your emotional energy without limitations from maladaptive energies and feelings. It also helps you learn about the importance of exercising the right judgment. Remember, your ultimate goal is to adhere to the principles of Ma'at, which will require you to impose judgments on your decisions, too, and not just on everyone else's.

Together, Chesed and Gevurah balance each other out. They also constantly influence each other, which you can use to your advantage. When you feel ready to expand your emotional energies, crossing through one and then the other sefirot will give you the balance you need to create a spiritually advantageous emotional landscape. Why is powerful emotional energy crucial for spiritual advancement? Its balance allows you to love freely without restraint, extending compassion and kindness to everyone and everything. It also gives you control over the emotional and spiritual goals you want to pursue or disregard, depending on what would help you advance faster.

Tiferet

To ensure you'll be able to absorb the energy of the loving union of Chesed and Gevurah, after Gevurah, you'll cross to Tiferet. Symbolizing beauty, Tiferet brings together two opposing forces. It's what allows you to form judgment with compassion, as passing one without compassion would go directly against the principles of Ma'at. Without Tiferet, there would be no true balance, and all judgments would likely be compassionless. This would hinder the ascension of every soul toward enlightenment. The beauty of Tiferet lies in its ability to hold you back from jumping to punishment right after judgment, without considering mercy. If you notice you've started taking a more tempered approach to situations where you need to pass judgment, this is a good sign you've ascended to Tiferet. It may be listening to a friend who has hurt you, allowing them to tell their side of the story instead of judging them for hurting you, as you would've done before. Strong connections foster powerful feelings, which can make it harder to avoid judgment without compassion. If you're able to hear out a very good friend who has hurt you, you're likely forming a powerful and balanced emotional, energetic landscape.

Instinctual Triad

Netzach

Symbolizing victory, Netzach is associated with the energy of endurance and perseverance. It's also connected with mercy, which can fuel your endurance by encouraging you to be compassionate to yourself when you make a mistake or fail to conquer a challenge. Netzach encourages you to look beyond the surface. It teaches you that not everything is always as it seems, and this applies to failure, too. Your failure may only be an opportunity to show how you can persevere in other ventures. When you're ready to face the obstacles and channel your energy to overcome them, it's a sign you're in Netzach. A sign that you're becoming a more resilient version of yourself, someone who doesn't back down in front of challenges and grows while conquering the obstacles that hinder your way to unity with the divine.

Hod

Hod represents glory and surrender. Fueled by the skill of looking beyond what you perceive, you can start working toward overcoming the hindrances in your way. When you ascend to Hod, you learn how to achieve the goal of removing the obstacles. Each of the milestones you must reach to get there becomes illuminated one by one until you can clearly see the path to success. Likewise, Hod prompts you to acknowledge some hard truths. For example, if resolving your problem means you have to pivot on your way, traversing across this sefirah will help you accept this. It will allow you to let go of what doesn't work and embrace what does. The power of Hod lies in its ability to offer realistic perspectives. This sefirah is full of realistic sensations and experiences, which makes it easier to identify and acknowledge the truths.

Yesod

The last instinctual sefirah, Yesod, symbolized the foundation of all knowledge. When you reach it, you're ready to become part of a whole and determined to make changes for a better world. It's a level of spirituality where you become fully aware of your energy and wisdom, including everything you've learned throughout your journey across the previous sefirot. Yesod also represents an ultimate test of authenticity. Tying together the wisdom from Hod and the instinctual ability to look beyond the surface you picked up in Netzach, Yesod invites you to manifest your authentic power, which transcends challenges, failures, and every other obstacle you may face on your way. Moreover, Yesod transfers the energy from the upper sefirot (the ones toward the top/crown) to the last one, Malkuth. Readiness to embrace your power and use it to help others so you can, ultimately, become united with the divine means you're likely in Yesod, and about to transcend to the final level of spiritual evolution. You still have growth to achieve, but you know how much your foundations have changed already.

Malkuth

The root of the Kemetic Tree of Life is represented by Malkuth, the sefirah of sovereignty. This stage is also known as the kingdom of divine power, as this is where souls become united with the divine presence. Despite containing the energies of all the other sefirot, Malkuth can seem a little underwhelming. It's not glorious like the sefirot of victory or warm like Chesed. Its unassuming nature is what gives it its true power. It represents reality, which has a massive grounding effect. A big sign of reaching Malkuth may be the ability to ground yourself in every circumstance, no matter what emotions, thoughts, or situations you're experiencing. This is the ultimate goal when ascending the Tree of Life because centering yourself allows you to adhere to the principles of Ma'at wherever it takes you to do this. As the last stage on the journey, Malkuth is where you see the ideas you identified as having potential manifest themselves. It's where you can express every creative thought, emotion, and ability you've picked up on your journey. Ultimately, after doing this and achieving complete enlightenment through unity with the divine, you reach a level of spirituality where you'll be able to utilize the wisdom of the universe in all areas of life. It's not just about spiritual growth. It's also about pulling some of the divine energy into the human world and using a transformative journey across the Tree of Life to do so.

The Four Stages of the Path of Ascent

Ascending the Kemetic Tree of Life prompts several shifts of consciousness. When crossing to Keter, you transition from a basic spiritual consciousness to a higher one. Your journey to Tifaret will take you to a more emotionally oriented consciousness. When reaching Yesod, you shift again from the emotional to a lower consciousness. Finally, when ascending to Malkuth, you transition to confidence in life.

As you switch between these levels of consciousness across the path of ascent, you go through four stages:

1. **Awakening to the Self:** This prompts the process of recognizing the interconnection of life and the divine spark within. You go from noticing how everything works together and separately to embracing your connection to the divine energy – and the realization that by reuniting with the divine energy, you'll become even more aware of everything, aligning yourself to live life authentically.

2. **Purification and Discipline:** This stage involves practicing ethical living based on Ma'at. This is when you get the urge to work toward balance and a state of wholeness, both within you and amid the energies you interact with. You feel the need to apply discipline and boundaries and adhere strictly to the principle of Ma'at.

3. **Integration of the Neteru:** This is when you switch to cultivating the divine principles represented by the Neteru. You learn to rely on intellectual, emotional, and instinctual abilities and combine them to achieve your goals. You learn to deal with (and learn from) failures, embracing them as opportunities for spiritual growth.

4. **Spiritual Union:** The last stage is about achieving harmony with the divine will and becoming a vessel for divine purpose. As the ultimate reward for your hard work through the ascension, you get to enter into a union with the divine. This is when you reach a level of consciousness where you're able to transform your life in a way you want it to transform from then on.

While navigating these stages on the path of ascent, you'll encounter plenty of challenges. Remember, these are representations of Set, the necessary chaos designed to test your strength and resilience. They're not there to ensure you won't succeed. Quite the contrary, Set comes to make victory and the ultimate union possible. After all, without Set, there wouldn't be Ma'at. It may bring destruction, but what comes after only makes you stronger. Just like when a disaster occurs in nature. Nature rebounds after the devastation, stronger than it ever was before. Without destruction and chaos, it wouldn't have the opportunity to become stronger. Likewise, confronting the darker aspects yourself, with all their challenges, will make you stronger. When you face your fears, traumas, or any other obstacles hindering your emotional and spiritual growth, you work toward inner balance. When you achieve this balance, you become a more adaptable and resilient version of yourself.

Ascending the Kemetic Tree of Life

This meditation will take you on a more advanced journey of ascension through the Kemetic Tree of Life. Following it, you'll be able to connect with divine energy and admire the strengths and wisdom of each sphere/stage on the path across the Tree.

Instructions:
1. Find a quiet and comfortable space where you won't be disturbed.
2. Take a deep breath in through your nose and out from your mouth. Repeat a few more times until you feel yourself relaxing.
3. When you feel relaxed, imagine you're walking in a beautiful green field. Smell the freshness of the air, and breathe it into your lungs.
4. Feel the earth beneath your feet and allow yourself to connect with the nature around you. Allow yourself to become grounded and centered.
5. Suddenly, you see a majestic, radiant tree in front of you. Its roots are firmly grounded in the earth, and the branches extend to the universe.
6. Set the intention to truly connect with the tree. Take a step toward it. While you do, you notice several glowing spheres on the branches of the tree.
7. As you reach the tree, reach out with your hands as if to touch it. Connect with its energy and will yourself to the first sphere. See yourself floating in the sphere.

8. You can feel the sphere's radiant energy, along with the energies of the qualities it hides. You can harness them if you wish.
9. Similarly, explore the other spheres on the tree as well. As you ascend through them, meditate on strength, compassion, courage, and divine love. Embrace these qualities as you encounter them and aim to continue your journey without leaving them behind.
10. When you reach the last sphere, you suddenly encounter an energy that is so pure you know it must be divine. You see yourself being bathed in warm white light. This is the energy of Atum-Ra, the source of creation.
11. To unite with this magnificent energy, affirm your intention with the following sentence:

    "I am one with the divine. I embody light, love, and wisdom."
12. You can spend as much time with the pure energy as you wish. When you feel ready, descend back to stand in front of the tree. Allow yourself to disconnect from the tree's energy.
13. Feel yourself becoming grounded in nature again. Your energies will be different, so it may take longer to center and balance yourself. Take your time. Imagine that you're one with nature, just like the tree in front of you. Your roots run just as deep and are nurtured from the ground.
14. After grounding yourself, reflect on messages you may have received or insights you may have gained on your journey.
15. Slowly let the image of the tree and nature go and return to your present. Record what you've learned on a journey. Make sure to note any emotions or new thoughts that may emerge during or after the practice. You may not understand them now, but you can always revisit them later. With a fresh perspective, you may be able to understand them more and their significance on your spiritual journey.

Chapter 6: The Power of Sacred Egyptian Symbols

The ancient Egyptians were known for their sacred and powerful symbols. Each one has a different meaning and significance. They connect the physical world with the spiritual realm, strengthen your spirituality, help you understand universal principles, bring you closer to the divine, and align you with the Tree of Life's energy to receive its guidance and wisdom.

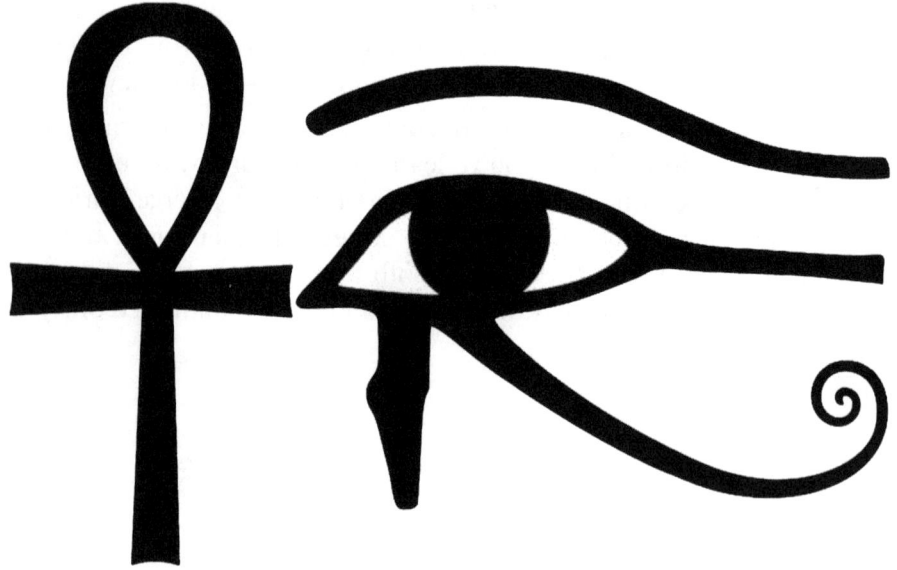

Ancient Egyptian symbols are known for their power and sacredness.[18]

This chapter explores various ancient Egyptian symbols and how they align with the energy of the Tree of Life and the spheres.

How the Tree of Life Embodies Universal Truths

The Tree of Life embodies universal truths and symbols that represent various meanings. Since it belongs to many cultures, the Tree of Life has come to be associated with different philosophies and religious beliefs. It shares its characteristics and other aspects with different civilizations. The Tree of Life symbolizes peace, rebirth, immortality, individuality, growth, strength, family, and ancestors. They are all universal truths that have governed humanity since the beginning of time.

Ancient Egyptian Symbols and the Spheres

Ancient Egyptian symbols can interact with the spheres and strengthen their spirituality. For instance, cosmic and creative forces flow through the ankh's sacred geometry. They amplify the spiritual energy of the spheres and reinforce their impact.

The djed pillar is another powerful ancient Egyptian symbol. It has regenerative and protective powers that can empower the spheres, making spiritual practices and energy work more effective.

The Ankh

The ankh is one of the most popular ancient Egyptian symbols. It is even a common jewelry design that many people wear worldwide, but only a few know its true meaning and power. The ankh is depicted as a cross but with a circle on top instead of a bar. It is also called the key of life, the key of the Nile, or the breath of life, and it symbolizes eternal life. This symbolism shows the ankh's connection to the upper or divine spheres and the Tree of Life.

However, life in this context doesn't involve one's mere existence. It also represents the immortal life the deities granted mankind in the afterlife. Horus, Anubis, and other gods and goddesses poured ankh streams over the bodies of the dead to symbolize eternity and life

The ankh, key of life.[14]

flowing from the divine to the deceased.

Historians believe that the Ankh is over 5,000 years old. It is also a hieroglyph that has three different sounds and is used in multiple words like "life" and "live," which represent the ankh's meaning. The ankh hieroglyph is also used in other words, like sandal strap and mirror.

In ancient Egyptian paintings, the ankh symbolizes life and all objects associated with it, such as water and air. It is also a symbol of power, and many gods and goddesses are depicted holding it to reflect their abilities in protecting life on Earth and bestowing the afterlife and paradise to souls after death.

On tombs, deities are shown placing the ankh over the deceased's mouths to revive them and return their soul and energy to their body to begin their journey in the afterlife. Here, it symbolizes the breath of life or air. It can also represent water, which was used in purification rituals, spiritual wisdom, the union of masculine and feminine energies, and the creation of life that resulted from this union.

The ankh is believed to be a combination of male and female symbols reflecting the marriage of Isis and Osiris. In ancient Egyptian mythology, the union between these two deities flooded the Nile every year. The water fertilized the lands and encouraged crop growth. This is why it's called the "Key of the Nile" and can also symbolize the unity of the physical and spiritual realms.

Ancient Egyptians incorporated the ankh in their amulets, mirror cases, jewelry, jars, fan bases, vessels, and many other artifacts. They even made flower bouquets that were shaped like the ankh and were given to the dead or made as offerings to their gods and goddesses.

Some Egyptologists think that it symbolizes the umbilical cord. It mirrors how life flows from the deities to humans, to how life transforms from mother to child. The umbilical cord was held in high regard in ancient Egyptian culture. In one story, children's umbilical cords were wrapped and preserved.

Many deities were depicted holding the ankh. However, it is mainly associated with Isis. In ancient Egypt's mythology, Isis gave the dead eternal life. According to the story, Isis brought her ankh close to Osiris's lungs and nose to bring him back to life.

The gods and goddesses held the ankh in many paintings, as it was the key to the spirit world. Some paintings show a person looking at the gods or the dead through the ankh's circle. This shows it was used to watch other realms.

The Role of the Ankh in Kemetic Rituals

The Ankh has been used in many spiritual practices to strengthen one's connection with the divine and the Tree of Life. You can meditate while holding the ankh to activate its energy force and harness its power. Choose a sacred place for meditation and add objects that represent the four elements (water, fire, air, and earth) and the four directions (south, north, east, and west). Hold the ankh with both hands, close your eyes, and imagine its oval part transforming divine energy into your body, bringing you balance and harmony.

You can also incorporate the ankh into breathing exercises. The circular part represents the breath of life. Place the ankh over your heart and take a few deep, slow breaths. Each time you inhale, imagine you breathe in life-giving energy through the oval shape. Feel it flow through your body, filling you with spiritual and mental clarity and good health. This can help you connect with the gods and the divine energy.

You can carry a small ankh in your wallet or wear it as a pendant to keep you connected with the divine and life force. Whether you are at work, with friends, or alone, you will be close to the energy of the universe, which will improve your physical, mental, and spiritual well-being.

Putting one next to your bed or under your pillow can encourage spiritual dreams. Spirits of your ancestors or deities may visit you to guide you or send you messages. Before bed, meditate on the ankh and ask the divine and the spirit guides to give you insight and signs in your dreams.

It can also be used in visualization. Close your eyes and imagine you are walking through an ancient Egyptian temple, and you find an ankh. You feel drawn to it and connect with it right away. You ask it questions, and it uses its knowledge of you and universal wisdom to guide you on your spiritual path and help you find your purpose in life.

The Feather of Ma'at

The feather of the goddess Ma'at is also called the feather of truth and is another significant symbol in ancient Egyptian mythology. It symbolizes universal harmony since it is associated with the goddess Ma'at and its concept. It is also connected to the Kemetic Tree of Life foundation, which was built on Ma'at's principles.

The feather of truth played an important role in the afterlife. The ancient Egyptians desired nothing more than to spend eternity in the Field of Reeds. It was a perfect existence, similar to their life on Earth, except there was no death, sadness, loss, pain, or diseases.

However, entering it required passing Osiris's trial. After a person died, their soul went to the Hall of Truth, where their heart was weighed against Ma'at's feather. If one's heart were heavier than the feather, it meant that they were bad, ungrateful, selfish, and sinful and should be punished for their actions.

However, if their heart was lighter than a feather, they were honest people and deserved to spend eternity in the Field of Reeds. A good person's heart is full of gratitude and is focused on the positive. They live according to Ma'at's principles and harmony, which the feather symbolizes.

Like Ma'at, the feather symbolizes justice and truth. It is depicted as a long ostrich feather with its tips bent over under its weight. The feather was also associated with Shu, the god of the air, Nut, the goddess of the sky, and Geb, the god of the earth. Shu was often depicted with a feather in his hair, and Geb dressed in feathers to symbolize the air that covers the earth.

The Role of the Feather of Ma'at in Kemetic Rituals

You can set up an altar and place a statue or images of Ma'at, an ostrich feather, or pictures or statues of the feather of truth, and an image or a small statue of the Tree of Life. Pray or meditate next to the altar and ask Ma'at or the feather to bring harmony and truth into your life. You can also hold the feather and meditate on it. Close your eyes and ask for guidance and to restore balance in your life.

The Eye of Horus

The Eye of Horus is also called the all-seeing eye, Udjat, or the Wadjet, meaning "The whole one," and it is one of the most powerful symbols in ancient Egypt. It is depicted as the eye of a falcon with drawings to make it similar to a human eye.

It is an enchanted symbol that represents rejuvenation, health, and protection. Ancient Egyptians used the Eye of Horus for its protective powers. They made it into amulets and put it on the living for protection and on the dead to guide them on their journey to the afterlife. Many people still wear the Eye of Horus as pendants to protect themselves from evil spirits.

The eye of Horus.[15]

This symbol originated from the myth of Isis, Osiris, and Set. After Isis brought Osiris to life, he became the god of the underworld. Isis hid from Set and raised Horus alone. When Horus grows up, he is adamant about taking vengeance and making Set pay for what he did to his father.

Horus fought Set multiple times to win back his kingdom. However, Set is very strong, and during one battle, Horus loses an eye. Set tore it out, cut it into pieces, and threw them away.

In another myth, Horus ripped out his own eye and gave it to his father to help him rule the underworld. However, Osiris ate it and came back to life. Afterward, the eye came to represent resurrection and life.

In both stories, Horus lost his eye but was made whole again so he could rule Egypt. It was either Thoth, god of wisdom and magic, or Hathor, goddess of beauty and love, who used their magic to restore his eye. As a result, ancient Egyptians believed it was magical and had protective and healing powers.

The restored Eye of Horus came to be known as Wadjet and symbolized the return of order (Horus) after chaos (Set). It was also connected with the concept of Ma'at.

The Eye of Horus also represented the ancient Egyptians' mathematical knowledge. It is believed that when Set ripped out Horus's eye, he tore it into six pieces. The Eye of Horus symbol was made of six parts. Each part had a fraction as a unit of measurement. The teardrop is 1/64, the curved tail is 1/32, the left side of the eye is 1/16, the right side is ½, the eyebrow is ⅛, and the pupil is ¼. They add up to 63/64. The missing part reflects that nothing in life is perfect, even if it was made of magic. It also symbolizes Thoth's magical abilities.

The Role of the Eye of Horus in Kemetic Rituals

The Eye of Horus reflects the energies that align with the spheres of protection within the Tree of Life. The symbol is as popular today as it was thousands of years ago. Many still believe in its magical properties. Some cultures paint it on their boats and ships or wear it as pieces of jewelry for protection.

It is used in meditation to reinforce your spiritual connection. The Eye of Horus also symbolizes knowledge and can be used in visualization and other Kemetic rituals to give you insights about your purpose and future.

The Scarab Beetle

The ancient Egyptian scarab beetle has a rich and fascinating history. It symbolizes resurrection, regeneration, and life. The symbol was incorporated into religious practices, iconography, and art, reflecting its significance in ancient Egyptian culture.

The scarab beetle laid eggs in its dung, which fed the babies after the eggs hatched. Ancient Egyptians were fascinated by seeing the young beetles emerging from the dung. They didn't know that the female laid eggs first, and so the beetles became associated with self-creation or creation in general. As a result, the symbol is connected to Ra, who created himself and came to life by emerging from the mounds. However, this isn't the only similarity between the sun god and this ancient symbol.

The scarab beetle.[16]

Khepri, the god of resurrection, transformation, and rebirth, and Ra's helper - manifested into the scarab beetle. He was originally called "Kheprer," meaning the scarab beetle. The symbol came to be associated with Ra, and the scarab beetle was even depicted pushing the sun across the sky, representing new beginnings.

The ancient Egyptians believed that the sun died and was reborn/resurrected every day. The scarab beetle emerging from dung balls represented regeneration and was compared to the sun god's daily journey.

Like the Eye of Horus, the scarab beetle has protective properties and can protect people from diseases and death. Ancient Egyptians believed it could also give them the power of manifestation, growth, rebirth, resurrection, and eternity.

The living wore it as an amulet to ward off evil and bring them good luck. They also put it on the dead to protect them on their journey to the afterlife and help them in the next stage of their existence in the Field of Reeds. They also engraved the scarab beetle on many tombs around the country for protection.

The ancient Egyptians highly revered the scarab beetle. They used them in prayers and spells to help the souls overcome challenges in the afterlife and give them direction. It is believed that if the dead wore a scarab amulet, their hearts wouldn't testify against them before Osiris.

The Role of the Scarab Beetle in Kemetic Rituals

The Scarab Beetle reflects energies that align with the spheres of renewal and creation within the Tree of Life. You can wear it as a pendant or get it as a statue and hold it during meditation. It can help strengthen your connection with sphere three, which represents the life force of creation. You can add a scarab beetle statue or image to your altar to symbolize renewal and pray or meditate when you feel stuck or that your life is stagnant.

The Djed Pillar

The djed pillar symbolizes stability. It is depicted as a column with a wide base that narrows as you near the top. The symbol was featured on tombs, papyrus, and palaces. It was linked to Ptah, the god of art and creation, who later became known as Ra. Ptah was depicted holding a scepter, which combined the ankh with the djed pillar and was called "The Noble Djed."

Every year, the ancient Egyptians held a festival called "The Raising of the Djed Pillar." During the festivities, the people built a djed pillar and erected it using ropes with the help of the priests. This represented the crops emerging from the earth. Over time, it became a symbol of Osiris returning from the underworld and his victory over Set. The djed came to be associated with Osiris and symbolized the stability and power of the ancient Egyptian kingdom.

The Djed pillar.[17]

Ancient Egyptians also raised the djed pillar during the Heb Sed festival to restore the king's power. It symbolized order, stability, and triumph. The djed pillar also represented the presence of the deities in a person's life and the stability of life after death. The symbol made them feel safe, knowing that their gods and goddesses were always with them, providing guidance and protection in this life and the next.

The djed pillar symbolizes resurrection. Like Osiris, people's souls were brought back to life after death and spent eternity in the Field of Reeds. It reminded them that death wasn't the end but a gateway to another realm.

The djed pillar is believed to represent the trunk of a tree and Osiris's spine. According to the myth of Isis, Osiris, and Set, after Set threw Osiris's coffin into the Nile, it ended up in Byblos, an ancient city in Lebanon, and a sacred tree grew around the coffin. The Byblos king often admired the huge tree and ordered his men to cut it into a pillar and bring it into his palace, unaware that Osiris's dead body was inside.

When Isis found her husband's body, she removed him and reconstructed the pillar, turning it into a sacred object which became the djed pillar.

In other parts of the mythology, the djed pillar was a fertility pole made from sheaves and reeds and was used in many ancient rituals. Other stories connect it with Seker, the falcon god of the Memphite Necropolis. The djed pillar is also believed to support the sky.

Ancient Egyptians would recite a spell while putting djed pillar amulets on the spine of the dead or painting it on their coffins. This should help the deceased sit up and use their spine in the afterlife.

The Role of the Djed Pillar in Kemetic Rituals

The djed pillar resonates with stability and endurance, echoing the grounding provided by the Tree's roots in balancing the material and spiritual realms. It can be used in grounding meditations and visualizations. You can hold it while meditating or visualize it grounding you to Mother Earth. Since it symbolizes a tree trunk, you can use it to ask the Tree of Life for help, guidance, and stability.

Practical Exercises

Meditating with Symbols and the Tree of Life

Visualize symbols like the ankh or the djed pillar glowing within specific spheres of the Tree of Life during meditation. This helps align the symbol's qualities with personal intentions, fostering a deeper understanding of their spiritual power.

Instructions

1. Sit comfortably and close your eyes.
2. Hold a small djed pillar in your hand.
3. Take a few slow, long, and deep breaths.
4. Imagine you are walking in the Egyptian desert, and you see the Tree of Life standing tall. You move closer and see the spheres.

5. Think of the djed pillar in your hands and visualize it moving through the spheres.
6. Watch the pillar glow as it aligns with the sphere energies.
7. Use what you know about the pillar and make intentions that align with its qualities. You can say, "I intended to have a more stable life."
8. Believe that the pillar will bring stability into your life.
9. Feel your connection with it growing.
10. Stay with this feeling for a few minutes.
11. Take a few deep, slow breaths, slowly open your eyes, and return to reality.

Integrating Symbols into Daily Rituals

Place symbols such as the feather of Ma'at or the eye of Horus on your altar near a representation of the Tree of Life. This reinforces harmony, balance, and protection during prayers or reflective moments.

How to Build an Altar

Instructions:

1. Choose a space for your altar. Keep it away from children or pets so it won't be disturbed.
2. Cleanse the area to remove dark and negative energy. You can burn sage and use the smoke for the cleansing ritual.
3. While cleansing, repeat the intention you plan to use to connect with the Tree of Life, the divine, and ancient symbols to grow and transform your life.
4. If you set it up on a table or any other surface, cover it with a piece of cloth.
5. Gather the objects you will add to your altar. Think of your intention as you place each one.
6. Place the feather of Ma'at. (You can use an ostrich's feather, a statue, or a sculpture of the feather.)
7. Place the eye of Horus on the altar.
8. You can also add an ankh, scarab beetle, and a djed pillar if you like.
9. After you finish, take a few deep breaths and express your gratitude to the altar.

10. Don't neglect your altar, and use it every day for prayer, visualization, or meditation.
11. Keep it maintained and clean, and cleanse it regularly.

Symbol Journaling with the Tree of Life

Draw or sketch symbols while reflecting on their alignment with the Tree of Life. For example, you can explore how the scarab beetle's themes of renewal correspond with the energies of the Tree's lower spheres, grounding you in cycles of personal transformation.

Ancient Egyptian symbols are more powerful than one can imagine. They are thousands of years old and have been associated with various myths throughout the years. These symbols can be invoked with different deities, bring stability, protection, and balance into your life, and help you connect with the spheres and the Tree of Life. You can tap into their power through meditation, visualization, and other Kemetic rituals. Find a symbol or more that resonates with you and incorporate it into your rituals. You can also wear one as a pendant to connect you with the divine's energy.

Chapter 7: The Kemetic Tree of Life for Personal Growth

Now that you have learned about the Kemetic Tree of Life, understood the Neteru spheres, and discovered all the deities associated with the Kemetic philosophy, you can practice everything you have learned.

The Kemetic tree of life allows for transformation and growth.[18]

You will learn how to use the tree for personal transformation and growth, the impact of working with spheres, and how they can help you with modern-day problems.

Tree of Life as a Holistic System

The Tree of Life is a universal symbol that people with different backgrounds and beliefs use to connect with the divine and their higher self to transform their lives. Thanks to Carl Jung's work, the tree has been associated with psychology for years. Jung believed that it stands at the center of one's psyche, representing individuation and one's journey to self-realization and wholeness.

Nowadays, the Tree of Life has become a symbol of the holistic system. It is incorporated into meditation, visualization, and other holistic therapies. The Tree's image is used as a focal point to expand your consciousness and help you stay centered and grounded to Mother Earth. You can use it in various exercises to put your spirit, mind, body, and emotions in harmony and strengthen their connection to one another.

Using the Tree of Life as holistic therapy helps align your thoughts, behavior, and actions with your goals, fills you with positivity, and pushes you to change, grow, and transform your life.

The Interconnection of the Spheres

The 11 Neteru spheres are interconnected aspects of personal development. Working with one sphere can impact others and help you grow in other areas. For instance, sphere six is the manifestation of one's will. Each person is responsible for their actions, choices, and behavior. They are free to choose their path in life. One can either accept Ma'at's principles and the Divine law and live a fulfilling life or reject them and surrender to chaos, leading to a hard and unhappy life.

These choices can affect the other spheres, such as sphere one (your true self or essential nature), sphere eight (emotions), etc.

Moving Between the Spheres

You can't focus your efforts and energy on one sphere. You need to move between them to balance the spiritual and practical aspects of your life. If you only focus on one side, the other will suffer. Say you only meditate or visualize without working on improving your health or advancing your career. These areas of your life will deteriorate. The opposite is also true. Neglecting your spiritual side will make you feel lost and disconnected from yourself, and you will start questioning your existence and purpose in life.

Remember that ascending and descending the tree isn't just a spiritual practice. It's also necessary to find harmony in your life. You need to create a balance between working on your higher self and spirituality while staying grounded in reality.

The Sphere and Modern Challenges

While the concept of the spheres was created years ago when people had different needs and aspirations, it is still relevant and can help you deal with and overcome modern challenges. For example, Sphere seven is responsible for your imagination and can help foster creativity. You can practice meditation or visualization techniques to connect with the sphere to help you tap into your creative side.

Sphere six is responsible for the manifestation of one's will and purpose. If you feel lost, you can connect with Horus and ask him to help you find your path in life.

If you want to build resilience, focus on sphere three and invoke Ra as the source of the life force. Ask him to give you the ability to face life difficulties with grace and the strength to overcome them.

Areas of Personal Growth

The Kemetic Tree of Life can help improve every aspect of your life. It can provide insights that help you understand yourself better so you can grow into the best version of yourself.

Boosting Your Self-Confidence

Many struggle with self-esteem problems. Thanks to social media, this issue has become more common. Nowadays, people feel pressured to have the perfect body, face, lifestyle, etc. When your Instagram friends are constantly posting pictures of their vacations, expensive clothes, and flawless skin, you can't help but compare yourself to them.

Oftentimes, you may have self-esteem issues because you have forgotten who you are and what you are capable of achieving.

Resilience

Life isn't without its challenges. You will face adversity and experience failures. Breakups, losing a loved one, financial problems, or career setbacks can turn your life upside down. Some people may struggle to cope with these situations. They may fall apart or suffer from mental issues. Unfortunately, not many are equipped with the skills to deal with tough times.

Resilience is your armor in life.[19]

Resilience can help you calmly face these situations, handle stress without breaking down, and recover easily.

Emotional Balance

If you don't control your emotions, they will take over and impact your actions, reactions, and behavior. People who have anxiety overthink every step they take and worry about every aspect of their lives, and those with anger problems lash out at others at the smallest inconvenience.

You need to be aware of your feelings at all times. Learn to release the negativity and embrace positivity. Validate your emotions and accept them to achieve emotional balance.

To overcome these issues and grow, you should meditate on the Tree of Life to discover traumatic experiences or childhood trauma that may affect your self-esteem, explore repressed emotions that cause emotional imbalance and impact your well-being, and tap into your skills and abilities to build resilience.

During meditation, use the tree for its guidance and wisdom. Invoke Ma'at's principles to bring harmony and balance into your life.

You can also practice visualization techniques where you imagine connecting with the tree so it passes its knowledge to you, or ask it questions that can help you heal and grow. Meditating on ancient

Egyptian symbols can restore your inner balance, keep you grounded, and strengthen your technique, making it more effective.

Connecting Ancient Wisdom with Modern Life

Ancient wisdom will always be relevant. You can use it to deal with many modern-day challenges. Invoke deities like Ra, Horus, or Osiris to help you overcome your fears, find your purpose, and navigate personal relationships.

Say you have a job interview. You are excited and hope you will get it. However, you're afraid you won't be able to answer all the interviewer's questions or that you don't have the skills to get the job. These fears can be crippling and stand in your way. You may be the right person for this vacancy, but you keep overthinking it or doubting yourself and miss your chance.

Before the interview, connect with nature and your inner self through meditation or visualization. Pray to an ancient Egyptian deity or the Tree of Life and ask it to calm your fears. Visualize that the tree of life extends one of its roots to you and absorbs your fears, leaving you confident, strong, and ready to tackle whatever life throws your way.

Many people live and die without finding their purpose. They look for something that excites them and makes them feel alive but fail. The Tree of Life holds all the answers you seek. Visualize asking it to help open your eyes and senses to know why you are here and what you are meant to do.

If you are having relationship problems, call on Ma'at to restore balance and harmony in your relationships.

Practical Exercises

Tree of Life Self-Reflection Exercise

Map out where you are on the Tree of Life by identifying which spheres resonate with your current life challenges or strengths. View your current life as a reflection of the Tree's balance. Journal on questions like: "Where in my life do I feel grounded, and where do I feel unsteady?" "What is one 'higher' quality I want to cultivate more?" Identify areas where you feel disconnected and use the Tree as a framework for realignment.

Balancing the Spheres

Use this self-assessment activity to evaluate how balanced you feel in the different areas of the spheres.

1. Do you feel grounded (first sphere)?

_____

_____

2. Do you feel connected to divine wisdom (second sphere)?

_____

_____

3. Do you feel emotionally balanced (fourth sphere)?

_____

_____

4. Do you feel aligned with higher wisdom (seventh sphere)?

_____

_____

5. Can you express your emotions easily and freely (eighth sphere)?

_____

_____

6. Do you feel aligned with your higher consciousness (tenth sphere)?

_____

_____

Focus on one underdeveloped sphere, creating small daily practices (e.g., acts of compassion for the sphere of love).

Harmony Practice

Use this daily practice to envision the Tree as a glowing force within you, connecting your physical, emotional, and spiritual energies. Take 5–10 minutes daily to focus on your internal "roots" (stability) and "branches" (aspirations).

Instructions:
1. Sit comfortably in a quiet place indoors or outdoors.
2. Take a few long, deep breaths. Inhale through your nose and exhale through your mouth.
3. Clear your head and relax your body.
4. Close your eyes and imagine you are walking in a beautiful green field.
5. Feel the grass beneath your feet and the breeze as it blows through your hair, listen to the birds singing in the sky and connect with your surroundings and Mother Earth.
6. Let go of everything, and allow your soul to guide you. Feel the energy of the trees around you and how they fill you with peace and tranquility.
7. As you walk through the forest, you see a glowing light at a distance. You feel drawn to the light and walk towards it.
8. The closer you get to the light, the dimmer it gets, and you can see what's under it. It is the Tree of Life. It is very tall, going up to the cosmos, and its branches extend to the sky.
9. Ask the tree if you can connect with it to feel its energy and wisdom flowing through you. Walk to the tree and notice how your connection grows stronger.
10. Place your left palm on the tree and connect with its heart. Imagine a line coming from its heart and connecting to yours.
11. You feel one with the tree. It is part of you, and you are part of it.
12. Feel the roots coming out of your feet, grounding you to the earth and nourishing your soul. They give you stability that can help you with any storm. Allow Mother Earth to fill you with its eternal love.
13. Now, connect with the tree's branches that extend to the sky and the cosmos. Allow them to connect you with the Great Spirit and the spirit guides of the ancient Egyptians.
14. They can guide you when you need help and give you insight into any situation. You can call on them whenever you need them and connect with the tree's wisdom.
15. Now, thank the tree for its help, take a few deep breaths, slowly open your eyes, and return to reality.

The Tree in Decision-Making

Approach a current decision or problem using the Tree as a guide. For example, you can reflect on how the decision aligns with the grounding stability of the base sphere, the creative vision of the higher spheres, or the wisdom of the divine. Use these journaling prompts to help you.

1. Does this decision honor your values and truth?

___

2. What energy from the Tree do you need to draw upon to move forward?

___

3. How will this decision benefit you?

___

4. How does this decision honor your long-term goals?

___

5. Will this decision bring order or chaos into your life?

___

6. How will this decision impact your life five years from now?

___

7. How can the Tree of Life help you with making the decision?
_____
_____
_____

8. What fears or doubts are preventing you from making a decision?
_____
_____
_____

9. How can the Tree of Life empower you and help you overcome your fears?
_____
_____
_____

10. Which past experiences or traumas are making you anxious?
_____
_____
_____

11. How can the Tree help you reflect on the past and deal with your issues?
_____
_____
_____

12. Is this decision moving you closer or away from your purpose?
_____
_____
_____

13. How do you feel about these decisions? What are these feelings trying to tell you?
_____
_____
_____

14. Does this decision align with your true self?

Problem-Solving with the Tree

Visualize a life challenge as if it's placed at the center of the Tree. Approach the problem from a "grounded" perspective (practical solutions) and a "higher" perspective (spiritual insight). Use these journaling prompts to help you integrate both views and identify actionable steps.

1. Think of the last time you overcame a challenge or solved a problem. How did you do it? What skills did you use that helped you solve it?

2. Break the problem into small parts. Which part can you solve first?

3. Think of a situation when you had to make a tough decision. What did you choose, and what was the outcome?

4. How do you overcome setbacks and failures?

5. Think of a time when things didn't go as planned. Did you feel that a higher power was pushing you in a different direction?

6. Have you faced a similar problem before? What lessons have you learned from it?

_____

_____

_____

7. Why do you think the universe is putting you through a similar situation? Does it want to teach you something new? Perhaps you haven't learned your lesson and are given another opportunity. Reflect on these questions.

_____

_____

_____

8. How can the Tree of Life give you insight to solve your problem?

_____

_____

_____

The Tree of Life Exercise for Building Self-Esteem

This simple technique will help you self-reflect and discover amazing abilities to boost your self-esteem.

Draw the Tree of Life

Get a large piece of paper and draw the Tree of Life. Your drawing doesn't have to be perfect. No one else will see it but you. However, you need to make it detailed. Include the roots, branches, leaves, grass, etc. Print one online if you can't draw. Just make sure it's large.

The Grass

Write down on the grass all the things that hold you back and prevent you from believing in yourself, such as an abusive childhood or relationship that destroyed your self-confidence or beauty/cultural standards that made you question your looks or skills. You should also write down the negative thoughts you have about yourself and the experiences, places, people, etc., that contribute to your self-esteem issues.

Write to the grass about your challenges.[20]

The Roots
Write down the roots of your country, hometown, family, school, culture, etc. You need to understand your experiences growing up and what shaped your youth to find the roots of your self-confidence issues.

The Ground
Write down the things you do daily or weekly as a result of your low self-esteem. For instance, you may put on makeup because you are uncomfortable with your looks or edit your pictures before posting them online. You should also add the bad habits that stem from your low self-confidence, such as exaggerating your achievements or constantly talking about yourself.

The Trunk
Reflect on your skills, abilities, and all the qualities you admire about yourself, and write them on the tree's trunk. If you struggle to think of something, you can think of all your accomplishments or the compliments you have received over the years.

The Branches
Write down your goals, dreams, and hopes on the branches. Don't hold anything back. These can be personal or professional. You should add all the goals you don't believe you have the skills for or can achieve.

The Leaves

Write down the names of friends, family, co-workers, and all the positive people in your life who make you feel good about yourself. Think of the ones who support you, lift you up, and make you believe in yourself.

The Fruits

Reflect on all the times you have made a difference in someone's life and write them down. Perhaps you have helped a friend through a bad breakup, stood up for your values, or rescued a sick dog. You have had an impact on many people's lives, even if you can't see it. Think of all the moments you have made someone's life better or done good deeds. If there is no space on the tree to write this part down, you can draw fruit baskets and write on them.

Tree of Life Letters Exercise

This exercise will help you reconnect with your inner self and the Tree of Life and gain a new perspective on yourself and your life.

1. Find a quiet room and lie down or sit comfortably.
2. Take a few slow, deep breaths and prepare yourself for the journey. Be still and close your eyes. Imagine you are lying down under a large tree.
3. You feel comfortable above the soft green grass and the beautiful, colorful flowers around you.
4. Look up at the sky and see the sun's rays coming through the tree's branches. The wind is blowing the leaves, and you watch them flying far away. You feel at peace.
5. One leaf falls off the tree slowly. You observe it as if you are watching a scene in slow motion. As it falls on your chest, you notice it is the shape of an envelope.
6. You hold the envelope-shaped leaf and notice how it feels in your hands. You see something written on it. You read the words, and it says, "Be present."
7. You listen to what the Tree tells you, and you start paying attention to your surroundings. You notice that the forest is very quiet, with only the occasional sound of birds in the distance.
8. You feel relaxed for the first time and mindful of your surroundings. Finally, you understand the power of being

present. You wonder why you haven't experienced this feeling before.
9. You understand that the Tree of Life wants you to be more observant, as this is the only way you can learn about yourself and the world.
10. As you enjoy the peacefulness of being present, the tree sends you another envelope-shaped leaf. You open it, and it says, "Self-love." Reflect on what these words mean to you.
11. You wonder if there are areas in your life where you could practice self-compassion.
12. Do you have goals you think you can't achieve? The Tree wants you to know that self-love isn't just about loving yourself but also about pushing yourself to achieve your goals.
13. You should take steps to build the life you have always wanted. All you need is self-love.
14. You also need to practice tough love to discipline yourself and push yourself out of your comfort zone.
15. You feel everything is quiet again. The Tree sends you another message. You open the leaf-shaped envelope, and it says, "Positivity."
16. You reflect on your life to see which areas require you to be more positive. The tree wants you to be positive during your darkest times. Positivity can boost your self-esteem.
17. The tree sends you another message. You open it, and it says, "Believe in yourself." You feel stronger than before. All the previous messages filled you with hope and self-belief. You decide that you want to live differently.
18. You will start to believe in yourself more. Believe that you can let go of self-doubt and grow. Let go of your anxiety and embrace who you can be.
19. Look at the sky and see how the Tree of Life is almost touching the clouds.
20. You are excited about your next chapter and the positive transformation coming your way.
21. Take a few deep breaths and slowly open your eyes.
22. Express your gratitude for the tree and reconnect with reality.

The Tree of Life is your teacher and guide. It can help you become resilient, confident, and strong enough to overcome your fears. Practice the exercises in this chapter every day to strengthen your connection with the trees and spheres.

Chapter 8: Reawakening the Tree of Life in Modern Times

Once a powerful symbol of metamorphosis, the Kemetic Tree of Life was an integral part of individual and community lives. While the practice of adhering to the Tree's principles may not be as popular as it once was, there is still a lot you can do to keep it alive within your life and that of your community. This chapter offers guidance on how to harness the Tree's ancient wisdom in modern times and explains why aligning yourself with the timeless values of the Tree of Life can be beneficial for growth, harmony, and spiritual enlightenment. Reading it, you'll find practical exercises for individuals and groups, as well as methods for extending the spiritual gifts you received to others.

Harness the Tree's ancient wisdom in modern times.[21]

The Enduring Relevance of the Kemetic Tree of Life

The modern world is often chaotic and designed to disregard personal values. Instead of creating communities based on shared goals and values, it erects a divide between individuals, hindering them from finding others with whom they could share their goals and values. In this chaos-ridden world, people need a counterbalance, something that can help them reconnect with their own values, as well as the shared ones. Many have found the solution to this by following the principles of the Tree of Life.

If you remember, the Tree of Life is closely associated with the principles of Ma'at, which is brought on by the aftermath of chaos. Therefore, the universal principles of the Tree can be the perfect counterweight to every challenge brought on by modern times. Moreover, these principles transcend time and culture. They are the same as they always were. They never change. Not with the trends, not from one society to another, nor are they affected by the mixing and matching of cultural ideologies that have transpired across time and space in history.

In a world where convenience leads to disconnection, embodying the Tree's principles can bring you back to your roots and transform your life into a thriving and purposeful existence. Just like in ancient times, individuals find adhering to the Tree's teachings highly beneficial to growth. Instead of being constantly tied down in the digital world, scrolling, checking balances, chasing numbers, keeping up with trends, and doing everything but connecting to others and themselves, the Tree allows them to slow down, disconnect, and just be. Be themselves by getting to know their dreams, the skills they want to hone, the goals they want to pursue, and the passions that drive them. Be with others by seeking out ways to nurture their connection with their communities, do something to make a difference, bring harmony to the life of the community, and much more.

While modern times have brought many freedoms, including the expression of different viewpoints about the various aspects of life, this has pushed universal truths into the background. These truths, born out of the laws of the universal divine energy of the creator, have always been present and served as a guiding star for many across history. Losing sight of them has often been shown to cause confusion and an even wider disconnect between individuals and their surroundings. However, did you know that the Tree of Life can also be used as a framework for rediscovering and aligning yourself with the universal truths? Each principle, quality, and energy represented by the Tree is based on universal truths. By reawakening the Tree within you, you bring these truths closer to the surface – and, in turn, they will encourage you to nurture a deeper connection with yourself, your community, and the divine.

The ancient teaching of Ma'at still resonates with many today, and this is particularly noticeable in modern movements that emphasize community building, eco-conscious behavior, and mindfulness. The principles of justice, order, balance, and truth are applied in all of these. For example, many contemporary Ma'at-based mindfulness practices focus on reaching a level of calm and focus where practitioners can channel the ancient energy of Ma'at and use it to harmonize their body, mind, and soul. Likewise, in a world of confusing ethical guidelines and rising needs to make righteous choices, many find guidance in the age-old teaching of the Tree of Life. In the same way it provides balance and stability, it can also show you what's right and what's wrong to do in every situation.

While sustainability is a relatively new concern, the core principles of sustainable practices are built on are not. Much of it comes down to balance. People have been altering the balance in nature with their behavior for the longest time. Eco-conscious and sustainability-driven initiatives seek to restore this balance and give back some of the blessings people have been receiving from nature since their creation. This growing desire for sustainable living in interconnected communities where people work toward common goals shows a stark parallel to Kemetic values. Living and working together requires trust and justice to keep order. Justice (with compassion), alongside honesty and universal truths, is deeply interwoven into the lives of sustainable communities. It's what helps them maintain balance in their lives, just as it did for the followers of Kemetic principles for centuries in the past.

Another idea for aligning with the Tree's principles on a community level is to form a "Living Tree." This Tree consists of people practicing the Tree's teachings. They act as branches of the Tree of Life, each of them contributing to community transformation and growth. The beauty of a Living Tree is that it can be as big as its members want it to be. The bigger it is, the more individuals can contribute to its expansion and transformation. If it gets big enough, collecting enough people to contribute to the same mundane and spiritual goals, it can even lead to a broader, global-level transformation. Each branch of the Tree has its responsibilities, including pursuing justice, balancing, and, naturally, adhering to the principles of Ma'at.

In the same vein, individual practitioners also have the responsibility to seek harmony and justice with compassion. In other words, if you have hopes to ascend the Tree of Life and reach spiritual enlightenment and unity with the divine, you should aim to moderate your influence on your environment. This requires a profound commitment, but the results of living authentically and responsibly will garner immense benefits for you and those around you.

Personal Commitment Ritual

Suppose you're wondering what the best way to show commitment to the principles of the Tree is. In that case, the answer is simple: by reawakening the energy of the Tree with you. You can do this by regularly performing a small ritual. It doesn't have to be extensive, nor do you need many objects for it. You can simply gather a symbol of the Tree, a candle, and/or incense to foster a calming atmosphere and focused mindset, and perhaps your journal to record any insight that may arise within you during the ritual. Having gathered this, you can proceed to perform a ritual like the one described below.

Instructions:
1. Light a candle and take a few deep breaths to relax. Do this in a quiet place where you won't be disturbed (for example, in a corner of your bedroom). You can also light the incense of your choice or put on meditative music. The goal is to completely relax your body and mind so you can properly focus on showing your commitment to the Tree.
2. When you feel sufficiently relaxed, tap into your energy. Feel it coursing through your body. Visualize your body lighting up with bright light.
3. Suddenly, in the center of your energy, you notice a warm glow. The glow starts spreading up and down, just like the branches and the roots of the tree extend up to the heavens and down to the ground.

4. As you visualize this Tree glowing within you, state an affirmation of your intention to embody the Tree's principles. For example, you can say something like this:

   "I am a vessel of harmony, growth, and enlightenment. I honor the wisdom of the Tree and bring its principles into my daily life."

5. Sit with your intention for as long as you wish, breathing deeply and revering the Tree's energy within you.

6. Once you're ready, let go of the image of the Tree. You can now record your experience. How did you express your intention to live in alignment with the Tree's values? How does expressing this make you feel? Did it make you feel more reassured or balanced?

7. When recording your experience and intention setting, focus on various areas of your life. It's a good idea to repeat this ritual at least once a week so you can focus on a different aspect every time you do it. For example, one week, your intentions can revolve around fostering love and compassion in your relationship; the next, it can switch to encouraging personal growth, while in a third week, you can set an intention to contribute to your community. After setting each intention, don't forget to record and contemplate how you can manifest it.

The Tree of Life Action Plan

The Tree of Life can be a blueprint for the goals you want to achieve. To use it in this aspect, you need to create a map based on the Tree's principles, then tie these to the different aspects of your life. Each principle can be associated with the parts of the Tree. For example, the roots can represent grounding and stability, the trunk growth and resilience, the branches expansion and purpose, the fruit, something you can give back, while the leaves can be reserved for love and compassion. This is optional, but you can also add other aspects and tree parts like fallen leaves to represent what you want to release – or even the ground to reinforce your grounding and self-empowering efforts.

Connect the tree of life to parts of the tree, like the roots and the trunk."

What do you need to make your action plan? You need a representation of the Tree of Life. This can be a large printout of the Tree, or you can draw a large tree by yourself based on how you usually imagine the Tree of Life when attempting to connect with it. You can draw each part as you like, including how big you want the branches to be, how deep you want the roots to go, how many fruits you want it to bring (if you want lots of them, you can also add baskets to represent the fruits you collected), etc.

Once you have your tree in front of you, set the intention to map it out based on the principles of the Tree of Life:

- **Ground (if you're adding it):** What can I do to ground myself profoundly and regularly? Add everything you do to center yourself, no matter how small this action may be. Little by little, they add up and will reinforce your equilibrium and spiritual power.
- **Roots:** Where do I find grounding and stability? Spend some time coming up with ideas for focus-supporting grounding. It can be a practice, affirmative statements, positive beliefs you adopted from your culture, mentors, etc. (you can recite these beliefs just like other affirmative statements).

- **Trunk:** What supports my growth and resilience? Curate a list of skills you've acquired or which you are currently working on honing to use in the future. Think of how you can use these to grow and become a more adaptable and resilient version of yourself.
- **Branches:** How do I expand my reach and express my purpose? What are your hopes and dreams for yourself? What about others? How do you wish for your community to improve?
- **Fruits:** What am I giving back to the world? Write down what you feel you've learned and what may allow you to help others. It may be someone else helping you by teaching you something important, and now you have the opportunity to leave a legacy by handing down the same knowledge to someone else.
- **Leaves (if you want to add them):** In what ways can I express love, compassion, and understanding to others and myself? Think about everyone you appreciate (including yourself) and how you can show them love and kindness.

When mapping out the Tree, write the answers to these questions on the appropriate tree parts. Use as few words as possible so you can have space for everything. Once you've mapped out your tree, it's time to create an action plan for every level. For example, to connect with the roots, you can commit to a regular mindfulness practice. Indulging in creative self-expression may be a great way to improve the branch aspects. Or, to connect with the fruits, you can start giving back by engaging in community service. Think of what actions you can take to harness the energy of the other tree parts as well.

Community Tree Meditation

Do you know what's even better than a connection to the Tree of Life through meditation? Sharing this transformative experience with others. If you have other people in your community who wish to join you on your journey, you can all get together and do a community meditation with the Kemetic Tree of Life. You can offer to host this event in person or even online if this is more convenient for all of you.

Instructions:

1. Everyone should gather in a quiet space or their respective spaces if hosting online. They should also have a representation of the Tree of Life with them.
2. After an initial relaxation exercise (for example, deep breathing or focusing on a meditative soundtrack/music), the group can slowly proceed to make a connection with the Tree of Life.
3. Everyone should start by imagining a magnificent tree in front of them. It may look different to everyone, but this is all right. The goal is for each member of the group to let their imagination loose and visualize the tree in their own way.
4. The members should each form an intention to connect with the tree. Then, focusing on this intention, they should visualize making a connection with it, becoming united with its energy.
5. Having united with the Tree's energy, each person should now imagine themselves as the extension of the Tree. For example, everyone can become a branch. As all branches of a tree are interconnected at some level, this will reinforce the community aspect of the connection you are all sharing with the Tree.
6. So, as you sit on the branches of this large tree, each of you contributes to the nourishment of the tree. You share a purpose and ownership over what you're contributing to the tree. Just like the spheres of the Tree of Life do.
7. Each participant should spend a little time contemplating their contribution. Then, when everyone feels ready to disconnect from the Tree, you can all let the image go. Again, this may take different amounts of time for each individual.
8. Finally, feel free to share your experiences. How did each of you imagine the Tree? How did you see yourself as interconnected as branches of a tree? How did each of you feel they contributed to the community? How can you contribute more to its harmony and growth?
9. Answer these questions and discuss your answers with the community. Together, you can find resolutions that will make your community stronger and contribute to each member's spiritual growth and balance.

End-of-Day Journaling with the Tree

Journaling is a wonderful way to organize and analyze your thoughts. It's also a transformative process leading to a profound relationship with yourself. In your journal, you can record everything that emerges from your mind and soul. As your thoughts and emotions fill the pages, the relationship deepens. When you incorporate the Tree of Life and its principles into this process, your journaling will gain a whole new meaning. For example, through an end-of-the-day journaling practice like the one below, you gain access to every aspect of your life, day by day. At the end of each day, you record something you experienced through the day and reflect on it. You'll have everything written down so you can remember how you felt and thought about your journey every day.

Journaling is a wonderful way to organize and analyze your thoughts.[28]

Journaling, instead of simple reflection, is also a powerful tool for eliminating judgment and criticism from your reflections. It lets you get as creative as you want to be, and it will only be you who sees the pages. You can be honest with yourself, which will contribute to your growth significantly. After all, you can only transform yourself if you know what needs to be transformed.

What do you need for journaling with the Tree of Life? You need a journal (a simple spiral notebook works fine, especially if you're a beginner), a pen or pencil, and a small representation of the Tree. For example, you can draw the Tree of Life on the first page of your journal. Or, you can have a small, flat pendant or symbol for the Tree and use it as a bookmark for your journal. Alternatively, you can simply keep a symbol near you on the desk or wall when journaling. Naturally, you'll also need a quiet space where you won't be disturbed.

Instructions:
1. Sit down with your journal and Tree of Life symbol in front of you, and take a few deep breaths to relax.
2. When you feel relaxed and your mind is focused on the task at hand, start reflecting by asking yourself questions like this:

   "Did I act with balance and harmony today?"

   "What energies of the Tree did I embody, and where can I improve tomorrow?"

   "How do I feel about my actions today?"

   "What are three things I feel grateful for having experienced today?"

   "Who did I help or make you feel appreciated today?"

   "What brought my spirit joy today?"

   "In what ways did I acknowledge and celebrate the teaching of the Tree today?"

   "What intention can I set to align with the Tree's energy tomorrow?"

   "Based on what I experienced today, how can I make a connection and gather knowledge from the tree tomorrow?"

   "What challenges did I face today when following the principles of the Tree of Life?"

   "Think of your future self, the person you seek to become. How would this person see and react to the experiences you had today?"

   "Think of a challenging or confusing situation you faced today. How did you handle it? Did you embrace the challenge and work through it? If yes, did this help you feel in harmony with the energies around you?"

   "What can I do before the end of the night to help me feel more aligned with the Tree?"

3. Write the first answer that comes to mind when answering these questions. Avoid contemplating whether it's the right answer or not. If it wasn't, you'll find out sooner or later, and this will be a great opportunity to learn from your mistakes and practice self-compassion.

Reconnecting with Nature

The Tree of Life offers a powerful connection to the natural world. The divine energy that it leads to is all around in nature. When you journey through the Tree, you take in nature and the divine energy it's infused with. This works in the opposite direction, too. By immersing yourself in nature, you'll find it easier to ascend the Tree of Life. This works best if you have the physical representation of the Tree - a real-life tree you find in nature. Why? There is a powerful symbolic connection between trees and the Tree of Life. Trees produce copious amounts of oxygen, the gaseous substance that sustains life. In other words, trees give life. They allow other life forms to grow and transform, just as the Tree of Life allows spiritual seekers to evolve by ascending it.

So, how do you reconnect with trees in nature? It's easy. Find the nearest patch of nature with trees in it. It could be in a park, a forest, or even trees in your backyard. Find a tree you feel drawn to. It will make it easier to align with its energy. When you find the tree you want to spend time with, simply sit under it and relax. You can do a full-on meditation or simply contemplate your connection with nature. For example, you can consider how the tree has grown over the years from a small sapling to its current size. Then, you can draw a parallel between the tree's growth and your own spiritual journey. The tree's growth was sustained by nature, and its energy was infused with divine essence. The spiritual growth you sustain is nurtured by the same energy. It infuses your root, just like it does with the tree, and provides strength for endurance and resilience to both.

If you find it challenging to draw parallels with a random tree, plant trees of your own. Tree planting in itself is one of the most powerful ways of building a relationship with nature. You give back, reciprocating the nurturing nature provided to you. Do this at the beginning of your journey, and you'll be able to track the tree's growth alongside your own progress.

If you don't have the means to plant trees, supporting ecological and/or sustainability initiatives is a wonderful alternative. It's another way of giving back and an extension of living the Tree's principles. Learning about the initiatives' purposes and workings often ignites a spark of creativity, which leads to innovative ideas from supporters of the initiatives. Besides letting you contribute to sustainability and lowering humanity's ecological footprint, the process also fosters a sense of ownership and pride. You learn to be compassionate, learn from mistakes, and understand what it takes to build a strong community that makes a difference in the world. It's just like traversing across the sefirot of the Tree of Life. It transforms your life and allows you to work on transforming others' lives, too.

Appendix: Kemetic Tree of Life Glossary

This chapter contains a glossary that encompasses all the terms related to the Kemetic Tree of Life and Kemetic Spirituality, as presented in this book.

A'aru - The ancient Egyptian term for the afterlife. (Chapter 3)

Ankh - The ancient Egyptian symbol of enduring life. (Chapter 6)

Atum-Ra - The father or king of the Egyptian gods, whose spiritual essence seekers aim to unite with by adhering to the principles of the Tree of Life. He is also known as the ancient Egyptian god of the sun. (Chapters 1, 2, and 5)

Ba - The ancient Kemetic term for the soul, the eternal essence that never dies.

Binah - The sefirah of understanding is the sphere where manifestation occurs, and ideas become reality. (Chapter 5)

Book of the Dead - The ancient text highlighting the symbolism of Ma'at (through depictions of scenes like the one in which the deceased's heart is weighed against the feather of Ma'at) alongside the importance of living a virtuous life. (Chapter 3)

Chesed - The sefirah of compassion and mercy provides opportunities for cultivating love or tumbling into love coming from others. (Chapter 5)

Chokmah - The sefirah of wisdom and the place for taking the essential oneness into tiny parts and analyzing the differences between them. (Chapter 5)

Da'at - The sefirah of knowing, which serves as a reminder that there are plenty of unknowns to be discovered. (Chapter 5)

Djed - A symbolic pillar representing Asar's spine, an ancient Egyptian symbol often associated with stability and endurance. (Chapter 6)

Eye of Horus - An ancient Egyptian symbol representing energies that align with the spheres of protection, renewal, and creation within the Tree. (Chapter 6)

Feather of Ma'at - An ancient Egyptian symbol for cosmic harmony, directly tied to the foundation of the Tree, which rests on the principle of Ma'at. (Chapter 6)

Geb - The manifestation of the Earth, representing sphere ten. (Chapter 2)

Gevurah - The sefirah of strength and boundaries is the sphere that teaches the limitations, along with the endings and boundaries, a person must set to be able to work toward spiritual growth. (Chapter 5)

Herukhuti or Ra-Horakhty - The representative of sphere five and karma and truth. (Chapter 2)

Hod - The sefirah of glory, which encourages understanding and learning what's beyond the surface and applying this knowledge. (Chapter 5)

Horus - The ancient Egyptian god of the sun, protection, and healing. He represents spheres six and seven. (Chapters 1 and 2)

Ife - A Ma'at philosophy that provides the understanding that all living creatures are connected on a deeper level. (Chapter 3)

Isis - The ancient Egyptian goddess of healing and the patron of divine motherhood. She represents sphere nine. (Chapter 1)

Ka - The ancient Kemetic term for the soul, the vital energy that encompasses everything and everyone made by the divine creator. (Chapter 2)

Kemet - The ancient name for Egypt, derived from the name for the black lands. (Chapters 2 and 3)

Kemetic Tree of Life - An ancient symbol that represents universal order and a guide for spiritual evolution. (Chapter 1)

Keter - The crown sitting on the very top of the Tree of Life, associated with divine energy. It helps understand the oneness of everything as it shows how the creator made everything work in unity. (Chapter 5)

Living Tree - The concept that refers to a community practice where each person who adheres to the teachings of the Tree of Life by embodying one of its branches contributes to a broader global transformation. (Chapter 8)

Maakheru - A Ma'at philosophy that dictates that everyone should align themself with cosmic truth. (Chapter 3)

Malkuth - The final sphere of the Tree of Life, sitting at the roots. As the ultimate destination during the ascent, it has a powerful grounding effect. It's also referred to as the realm of manifestation of the human world and all the people who live and die in it (Chapter 5).

Ma'at - The ancient Kemetic concept embodying the virtues of order, truth, justice, and harmony – the principles Kemetic Spiritual practices the Tree of Life are based on. Also mentioned as a goddess of justice, representing sphere four. (Chapters 1 and 2)

Mehen - A Ma'at philosophy dictating that everything should be in moderation and that people should avoid extremes to find harmony. (Chapter 3)

Neter (or Neteru in plural) - The ancient term for self-made divinity or gods/goddesses. In Kemetic Spirituality, Neteru are seen as manifestations of universal principles. (Chapters 1 and 2)

Netzach - The sefirah of victory is the place where individuals can surrender to transformation and the unknown truths are revealed to them. (Chapter 5)

Number One - The number symbolizes unity and Atum, the source of all creation. (Chapter 4)

Number Three - The number associated with the balance of creation, preservation, and destruction. (Chapter 4)

Number Four - The number symbolizing stability. It's also associated with Ma'at and the cardinal directions. (Chapter 4)

Number Seven - The number associated with spiritual completeness and cycles. (Chapter 4)

Number Nine - The number representing divine energy and the Ennead of Heliopolis. (Chapter 4)

Osiris - The ancient Egyptian god of resurrection, transformation, and, according to legends, the first king of Egypt. (Chapter 1)

Path of ascent - The term that refers to an individual's journey to higher consciousness, self-mastery, and unity with the divine. (Chapter 5)

Ptah - The creator god who, according to the ancient lore, ruled the central tree, which became known as the Tree of Life. (Chapter 1)

Rit - One of Ma'at's philosophies, teaching people to be respectful, appropriate, and dignified in every situation. (Chapter 3)

Sacred geometry - A Kemetic concept that reflects numerological principles and their alignment with the spheres on the Tree of Life, like triangles and pyramids. (Chapter 4)

Scarab Beetle - Another ancient Egyptian symbol reflecting energies that align with the spheres of protection, renewal, and creation within the Tree. (Chapter 6)

Sefirah (or sefirot in plural) - The term is used to represent the stages or stations on the tree of life. Each sefirot is associated with a quality and knowledge that can be harnessed. (Chapter 5)

Set - The ancient Egyptian god of chaos and challenge. He embodies the counterbalance to Ma'at and is considered necessary to be able to follow the principles of Ma'at. (Chapter 2)

Sobek - The crocodile god, representing sphere eight of the Tree. (Chapter 2)

Sokar - The god of the dead, representing sphere three of the Tree. (Chapter 2)

Spheres of the Tree of Life - These are structures that embody numerical principles that reflect stages of spiritual ascent. (Chapter 4)

Spiritual Union - The process that follows after reaching the end of the path of ascent (the last sphere on the Tree of Life), whereby a person can achieve harmony with the divine will and become a vessel for divine purpose. (Chapter 5)

Tiferet - The sefirah beauty represents an open heart, which balances what a person can offer to and accept from others, shaping their entire existence. (Chapter 5)

Tehuti - The spiritual master representing sphere two of the Tree. (Chapter 2)

Yesod - The sefirah of the foundation of all knowledge, including the knowledge hidden in the collective unconscious, the key to deciphering dreams and symbols that lead you to discover underlying patterns of everything happening around you. (Chapter 5)

Conclusion

Now that you have reached the end of this book, it's time to summarize what you've learned. The first chapter introduced you to the origins and key principles of the Tree of Life. You have also learned about the role the Tree played in ancient Egyptian spirituality, including its significance as a representation of universal order and a guide for spiritual growth and transformation. Then, you were able to explore the connection between the Neteru (the ancient gods associated with embodiments of divine energy or principles) and the Tree. You've seen how the Neteru are interwoven into the Tree's structure and symbolism.

Next, you've learned that the Tree of Life also shows a profound connection with Ma'at, the foundational concept in Kemetic philosophy. Representing truth, balance, order, and justice, Ma'at's teachings are deeply interwoven into the Tree's principles and the wisdom you can harness by connecting to it.

Chapter 4 showcased the numerical association of the Tree of Life, highlighting numbers with crucial significance to the Tree's principles. Just as this chapter offered some practical exercises to explore numerology further, the next one did the same with practices tied to the path of ascent. Here, you've also learned what hidden wisdom you can gather while ascending the various parts of the Tree. Commonly known as sefirot, the stages of the Tree of Life each contain valuable lessons with incredibly transformative effects.

The subsequent chapter expanded on the connection between the Tree of Life and the sacred symbolism that is found to complement its teachings. You've seen the role these symbols have played in ancient Egyptian culture, as well as in Kemetic spirituality, where they encode truths and principles and act as guides for aligning with the energy of the Tree. Here, you also found practical instruction for integrating symbols into your workings with the Tree.

The penultimate chapter was all about personal growth and using the Tree of Life to achieve this. From applicable techniques for self-reflection, harmony, balancing spheres, decision-making and problem-solving, the Tree can be a wonderful ally for all kinds of personal growth-inducing practices.

In the same vein, the last chapter showed you that the Tree can also be used to establish harmony within you and your community, effectively countering the harmful and chaotic effects of the fast-paced, modern world. By integrating the Tree and its principles into individual and group practices, you can awaken the Tree's energy within, reestablish harmony, and form a profound connection with yourself and those around you. Together, you can make a difference that contributes to the growth and transformation of the community.

Your journey through this book may be concluded, but your journey of navigating your spiritual growth while using the Tree of Life as a guide has just begun. May it be as transformative and fulfilling as you want it to be and bring you the enlightenment and spiritual elevation you seek.

If you enjoyed this book, I'd greatly appreciate a review on Amazon because it helps me to create more books that people want. It would mean a lot to hear from you.

To leave a review:
1. Open your camera app.
2. Point your mobile device at the QR code.
3. The review page will appear in your web browser.

Thanks for your support!

Here's another book by Mari Silva that you might like

Your Free Gift
(only available for a limited time)

Thanks for getting this book! If you want to learn more about various spirituality topics, then join Mari Silva's community and get a free guided meditation MP3 for awakening your third eye. This guided meditation mp3 is designed to open and strengthen ones third eye so you can experience a higher state of consciousness. Simply visit the link below the image to get started.

https://spiritualityspot.com/meditation
Or, Scan the QR code!

References

(2025). Twinkl.com. https://www.twinkl.com/teaching-wiki/the-tree-of-life-in-ancient-egypt

Ancient Egypt: the Mythology - Feather. (n.d.). Www.egyptianmyths.net. http://www.egyptianmyths.net/feather.htm

Ashby, M. (2021). The Kemetic Tree of Life. Blinkist. https://www.blinkist.com/en/books/the-kemetic-tree-of-life-en

Blackstock, J. (2025, February 20). The Tree of Life: A Universal Symbol of Growth, Connection, and Transformation. Taproot Therapy Collective. https://gettherapybirmingham.com/the-tree-of-life-a-universal-symbol-of-growth-connection-and-transformation/

Cassar, C. (2024, January 31). The 42 Laws of Maat: The Moral Principles of the Ancient Egyptians. Anthropology Review. https://anthropologyreview.org/history/ancient-egypt/42-laws-of-maat-principles/#The_42_Laws_of_Maat

Chariot to Heaven, Kemet. (n.d.). Www.griffith.ox.ac.uk. http://www.griffith.ox.ac.uk/gri/9kemet.html

Cherry, K. (2023, May 3). How Resilience Helps You Cope With Life's Challenges. Verywell Mind. https://www.verywellmind.com/what-is-resilience-2795059

Chestnut, K. (2024, March 22). Kemetic Spirituality: Egyptian Interconnection and Modern Practice - KatharineChestnut.com. KatharineChestnut.com. https://katharinechestnut.com/kemetic-spirituality-egyptian-interconnection-and-modern-practice/?srsltid=AfmBOorhKZBWb8nTq5-7-2idc7oPmqkzG9pSJpJ9UIaYQL9-tcb2kfHL

Chris. (2024, May 30). Personal and Spiritual Growth. Inner-Growth.info. https://inner-growth.info/wisdom-of-the-ages/ancient-wisdom/the-legacy-of-egyptian-mysticism-in-contemporary-spirituality/

Cleopatra Egypt Tours. (2020, April 8). Ankh Symbol - The facts & meaning of the Egyptian Cross. Egypt Tour Packages | Egypt Tours | Egypt Day Tours | Cruises in Egypt. https://www.cleopatraegypttours.com/travel-guide/the-egyptian-ankh-symbol-meaning/

dhwty. (2018, November 18). Eye of Horus: The True Meaning of an Ancient, Powerful Symbol. Ancient-Origins.net; Ancient Origins. https://www.ancient-origins.net/artifacts-other-artifacts/eye-horus-0011014

Digital Underground. (2022, May 23). The Tree of Life: Notes From The Digital Underground. Notes from the Digital Underground. https://notesfromthedigitalunderground.net/the-tree-of-life-2/

Divinesoulseekers. (2024, December 30). Messages in Numbers: Discovering Your Soul's Divine Blueprint. Medium. https://medium.com/@divinesoulseekers888/messages-in-numbers-discovering-your-souls-divine-blueprint-1e6be5544f92

Dr. Kwame Nantambu. (2025). trinicenter.com - Role of Numbers in Ancient Kemet (Egypt). Trinicenter.com. http://www.trinicenter.com/kwame/2002/Aug/

Egyptian Scarab (Dung beetle). (2020, April 15). Egypt Fun Tours; Fun Tours. https://egyptfuntours.com/blog/the-egyptian-scarab-dung-beetle/

ETP Team. (2025, April 27). Ancient Egyptian Principles of Maat: The Sacred Law of Balance, Truth, and Cosmic Order. Egypt Tours Portal. https://www.egypttoursportal.com/blog/ancient-egyptian-civilization/ancient-egyptian-princibles-of-maat/

Eye of Horus Symbol Meaning - Eye of Horus Facts. (2023, October 10). Trips in Egypt. https://www.tripsinegypt.com/blog/ancient-egyptian-civilization/eye-of-horus/

Eye Of Unity. (2024, February 9). Macrocosm and Microcosm: Bridging the Gap between Cosmic and Subatomic Worlds. Medium. https://medium.com/@eyesofunity/macrocosm-and-microcosm-bridging-the-gap-between-cosmic-and-subatomic-worlds-4d1945dc2ba2

Fares, A. (2020, July 20). The Ankh: An Egyptian Symbol for Life. Www.pyramidsland.com. https://www.pyramidsland.com/blog/the-ankh-an-egyptian-symbol-for-life

Fleur, P. (2024, July 8). How to use the Ankh in your Spiritual Practice. Prism + Fleur. https://www.prismandfleur.com/post/how-to-use-the-ankh-in-your-spiritual-practice?srsltid=AfmBOooh9dPx9418gT3HlKKJYqUgGRanHt-DsncUnr2-uBqgvshMnO7a

Gaeta, J. (2024, December 17). Creating a Holistic Lifestyle: The Beginners Guide. Becoming You with Julie. https://becomingyouwithjulie.com/creating-a-holistic-lifestyle-beginners-guide/

galina. (2024, January 21). Принципите на Маат. Universe Mind. https://universemind.info/en/printsipite-na-maat/

GatherTales Content Group. (2024, August 24). The Tale of Ma'at. Gathertales.com; GatherTales. https://www.gathertales.com/en/story/the-tale-of-maat/sid-258

Grabatin, E. (2024, October 29). 52 Journal Prompts for Making Decisions at Life's Crossroads -. Emily Grabatin - Non-Fiction Book Coach and Indie Publishing Coach for Faith-Inspired Authors. https://emilygrabatin.ca/journal-prompts-for-making-decisions/

Hagen, P. (2025). Journaling for Problem Solving: Effective Techniques and Prompts. Hagengrowth.com. https://hagengrowth.com/journaling-for-problem-solving/

Holysands, & Sharon, G. (2020, December 13). The Significance and Meaning of the Kabbalah Tree of Life. Holysands. https://holysands.com/the-significance-and-meaning-of-the-kabbalah-tree-of-life/?srsltid=AfmBOop0ok4vsPlCWtxfbTLPjPS9qIOTHgGL6hvVwe9lsSsqSI3Nb799

Insight Network, Inc. (2025). Insight Timer - #1 Free Meditation App for Sleep, Relax & More. Insighttimer.com. https://insighttimer.com/andybrine/guided-meditations/tree-of-life-guided-meditation

Insight Network, Inc. (2025a). Insight Timer - #1 Free Meditation App for Sleep, Relax & More. Insighttimer.com. https://insighttimer.com/andybrine/guided-meditations/tree-of-life-guided-meditation

Isidora. (2012, June 2). Isis & the Ankh. Isiopolis. https://isiopolis.com/2012/06/02/isis-the-ankh/

Jakada Tours Egypt. (2021, May 2). The Egyptian Scarab Beetle and Its Meaning | Scarab Symbol Meaning. Jakada Tours Egypt. https://jakadatoursegypt.com/the-egyptian-scarab-beetle-and-its-meaning/

Journey To Egypt. (n.d.). Www.journeytoegypt.com. https://www.journeytoegypt.com/en/blog/eye-of-horus

Kemet Experience. (2019, March 24). The 42 ideals of Ma'at. Kemet Experience. https://www.kemetexperience.com/the-42-ideals-of-maat/

Lin, A. (2023, April 30). The Tree Of Life: Symbolism And Its Meaning. Inner Wisdom Store. https://innerwisdomstore.com/blogs/guide/the-tree-of-life-symbolism-meaning?srsltid=AfmBOoovzWjzLedLP6A3WyyV4UqII0buDxO1cU02Q2hf Wai63L6pvXrz

Lloyd, A. (2024, January 9). Goddess Of Truth, Justice, Order, Harmony And Morality. Medium. https://medium.com/@annalloydc/goddess-of-truth-justice-order-harmony-and-morality-900ad2c011b5

Lor, H. O. (2021, September 24). The Tree of Life Symbol Meaning | House of Lor Pure Irish Gold Jewellery. House of Lor | Irish Jewellery | Pure Gold Mined in Ireland. https://houseoflor.com/the-tree-of-life-symbol/

Luuckk, L. (2024, July 11). Tree of Life and Meditation: A Spiritual Journey Towards Well-being and Healing. Luuckk. https://luuckk.com/en-en/blogs/articles/tree-of-life-and-meditation-a-spiritual-journey-towards-wellbeing-and-healing

Ma'at - (History of Africa – Before 1800) - Vocab, Definition, Explanations | Fiveable. (2018). Fiveable.me. https://fiveable.me/key-terms/africa-before-1800/maat

Mark, J. (2016, September 15). Ma'at. Www.worldhistory.org. https://www.worldhistory.org/Ma

Mark, J. (2016a, February 19). Isis. World History Encyclopedia. https://www.worldhistory.org/isis/

Mark, J. (2016b, March 6). Osiris. World History Encyclopedia. https://www.worldhistory.org/osiris/

Mark, J. (2018, March 30). The Egyptian Afterlife & The Feather of Truth. World History Encyclopedia. https://www.worldhistory.org/article/42/the-egyptian-afterlife--the-feather-of-truth/

Mark, J. (2021, May 20). Ra (Egyptian God). World History Encyclopedia; World History Encyclopedia. https://www.worldhistory.org/Ra_(Egyptian_God)/

Mark, J. (2016, March 3). Djed. World History Encyclopedia. https://www.worldhistory.org/Djed/

Mark, J. J. (2016, March 7). Set (Egyptian God). World History Encyclopedia. https://www.worldhistory.org/Set_(Egyptian_God)/

Markkula Center for Applied Ethics. (2021, November 8). A framework for ethical decision making. Santa Clara University. https://www.scu.edu/ethics/ethics-resources/a-framework-for-ethical-decision-making/

Masqueradetheheart. (2025, April 16). Ma'at - Egypt Museum. Egypt Museum. https://egypt-museum.com/maat/

Mendes, J. (2023, March 15). Jamen Mendes – My Spiritual Link to Ancient Egypt! - ILLUMINATION - Medium. Medium; ILLUMINATION.

https://medium.com/illumination/mendes-my-spiritual-link-to-ancient-egypt-137bd1bb71b4

Miller, L. (2021, May 12). Archetypes and the Egyptian Creation Story. ILLUMINATION. https://medium.com/illumination/archetypes-and-the-egyptian-creation-story-9a1a67d02a1e

Mohdatieq. (2023, February 13). The Paradox of Life as a Harmony of Chaos and Order. Medium. https://medium.com/@mohdatieq86/the-paradox-of-life-as-a-harmony-of-chaos-and-order-28b49cf9872c

Morgan, R. (2019, August 31). Sacred Geometry Art, Symbols & Meanings. Pardesco. https://pardesco.com/blogs/news/sacred-geometry-art-symbols-meanings?srsltid=AfmBOopSR1FUZAUA9o3d-eBrWb_hZS_Zeog4RzH7mD534_7mC7gRqjid

Morgan, R. (2023, March 28). Tree of Life. Pardesco. https://pardesco.com/blogs/news/tree-of-life?srsltid=AfmBOorxKs5I4vOmZeWBtMXTRdv40D5KHbuDhxQQ1FmrF0UoTnzaIXWd

Nabil, M. (2025). Role of Numbers in Ancient Kemet (Egypt). Scribd. https://www.scribd.com/document/125627372/Role-of-Numbers-in-Ancient-Kemet-Egypt

Napilay, J. (2024, August 8). How Ancient Myths and Legends Reflect the Societal Values and Beliefs of the Cultures That Created Them. Medium; Medium. https://medium.com/@joshuanapilay/how-ancient-myths-and-legends-reflect-the-societal-values-and-beliefs-of-the-cultures-that-created-8dc3bb1a926e

Nathan b. Weller. (2015, February 2). The Tree of Life: A Simple Exercise for Reclaiming Your Identity and Direction in Life Through Story - Nathan B. Weller. Nathan B. Weller. https://nathanbweller.com/tree-life-simple-exercise-reclaiming-identity-direction-life-story/

Neteru – The Divine Energies - Egyptian Wisdom Center. (2018, October 30). Egyptian Wisdom Center - Learning from Ancient Egypt. https://egyptianwisdomcenter.org/neteru-the-divine-energies-2/

Numbers as Symbols. (2010, February 28). Gospel Doctrine Daybreak 10th Ward. https://lds10.wordpress.com/2010/02/28/numbers-as-symbols/

Numerology Of The Creation Process - Egyptian Wisdom Center. (2018, October 30). Egyptian Wisdom Center - Learning from Ancient Egypt. https://egyptianwisdomcenter.org/numerology-of-the-creation-process-2/

Ouvry, T. (2023). Tree of Life Meditation – Toby Ouvry Meditation. Tobyouvry.com. https://tobyouvry.com/tag/tree-of-life-meditation/

Pardoel, J. (2021, November 9). The Spiritual Meaning of the Ankh. Sacred Creation. https://www.sacredgeometryshop.com/spirituality/the-spiritual-meaning-of-the-ankh/

RA Herukhuti. (2022, February). The Tree Of Life In Ancient Kemet. AfrikaIsWoke.com. https://www.afrikaiswoke.com/the-tree-of-life-in-ancient-egypts-metu-neter-explained/

Ramblings_Of_Ancient_Egypt. (2023, November 22). The Necessity for Balance | Mythology Journal. Medium; Mythology Journal. https://medium.com/mythology-journal/the-necessity-for-balance-f560bde9fdf6

Ramblings_Of_Ancient_Egypt. (2023, October 17). Journey of the Sun- Ancient Egyptian Myth | Mythology Journal. Medium; Mythology Journal. https://medium.com/mythology-journal/journey-of-the-sun-cb5eccdd4334

Reese, M. R. (2014, November 14). The Sacred Symbol of the Djed Pillar. Ancient Origins: Reconstructing the Story of Humanity's Past. https://www.ancient-origins.net/myths-legends-africa/sacred-symbol-djed-pillar-002325

Rise, R. &. (2022, February 16). 18 Journal Prompts for Reflecting on the End of the Day. Root & Rise. https://www.rootandriseblog.com/18-journal-prompts-for-reflecting-on-the-end-of-the-day/

Rosicrucian Egyptian Museum. (2019a). Isis - Explore Deities of Ancient Egypt. Egyptianmuseum.org. https://egyptianmuseum.org/deities-isis

Rosicrucian Egyptian Museum. (2019b). Osiris - Explore Deities of Ancient Egypt. Egyptianmuseum.org. https://egyptianmuseum.org/deities-osiris

Rosicrucian Egyptian Museum. (2019c). Seth - Explore Deities of Ancient Egypt. Egyptianmuseum.org. https://egyptianmuseum.org/deities-seth

Rosicrucian Egyptian Museum. (2022). Ma'at- Explore Deities of Ancient Egypt. Egyptianmuseum.org. https://egyptianmuseum.org/deities-Maat

Rosicrucian Egyptian Museum. (2024). Ra - Explore Deities of Ancient Egypt. Egyptianmuseum.org. https://egyptianmuseum.org/deities-ra

Rousselle, M. (2024, February 7). Balancing Order and Chaos is The Key to your Success. Medium; Bootcamp. https://medium.com/design-bootcamp/balancing-order-and-chaos-is-the-key-to-your-success-6a1f6705bb5d

Sacred Geometry & Numbers 101. (2018, December 3). The Eye of Ra. https://eyeofra.blog/2018/12/02/sacred-geometry-numbers-101/

Saleh, E. (2023, December 3). The Concept of Maat: A Source of Inspiration. Ebaalaw.com. https://ebaalaw.com/maatconcept/

San-Aset. (2017, October 12). The 42 Ideals of Ma'at. Iseum Sanctuary. https://iseumsanctuary.com/2017/10/11/the-laws-and-ideals-of-maat/

Sanders, D. (2024). Introduction to the Tree of Life. Kabbalah Experience. https://kabbalahexperience.com/introduction-to-the-tree-of-life/

Scarab Beetles, Creation and the Sun. (2021, May 7). Tales from the Two Lands; Tales from the Two Lands.

https://talesfromthetwolands.org/2021/05/07/scarab-beetles-creation-and-the-sun/

Sims, K. (n.d.). Finding Emotional Balance. Birch Psychology. https://www.birchpsychology.com/birchs-blog/finding-emotional-balance

Singer, J. W. (2021, May 9). Book of the Dead of Hunefer: The Judgement Scene | DailyArt Magazine. DailyArtMagazine.com - Art History Stories. https://www.dailyartmagazine.com/judgement-scene-hunefer/

SparkNotes. (2024). Kabbalah: The Ten Sefirot Summary & Analysis | SparkNotes. SparkNotes. https://www.sparknotes.com/philosophy/kabbalah/section6/

Spearman, L. W. (2025). The Kamitic Tree of Life. Scribd. https://www.scribd.com/doc/29625398/The-Kamitic-Tree-of-Life

Team, E. (2019a, September 10). The Djed Pillar. Egypt Tours Portal. https://www.egypttoursportal.com/en-us/the-djed-pillar/

Team, E. (2019b, September 11). Egyptian Scarab Beetle. Egypt Tours Portal. https://www.egypttoursportal.com/egyptian-scarab-beetle/

The Tree of Life: A Simple Exercise for Reclaiming Your Identity and Direction in Life Through Story - Nathan B. Weller. (2015, February 2). Nathan B. Weller. https://nathanbweller.com/tree-life-simple-exercise-reclaiming-identity-direction-life-story/#The_Tree_of_Life_Exercise

Tukios Websites. (2024, May 17). Embracing Life by Embracing Death: Understanding the Death Positive Movement. Newcomergreenbay.com. https://www.newcomergreenbay.com/embracing-life-by-embracing-death-understanding-the-death-positive-movement

van Blerk, N. (2018). The Emergence of Law in Ancient Egypt: The Role of Maat. Fundamina, 24(1), 60–88. https://doi.org/10.17159/2411-7870/2018/v24n1a4

We'Moon. (n.d.). Understanding Altars: What is an altar, and how to bring altar magic into my life. We'Moon. https://wemoon.ws/blogs/magical-arts/understanding-altars-what-is-an-altar-and-how-to-bring-altar-magic-into-my-life

What is the Tree of Life - Everything You Need to Know About Its Meaning and Symbolism. (n.d.). Dublez.com. https://www.dublez.com/what-is-the-tree-of-life-everything-you-need-to-know-about-its-meaning-and-symbolism-a16?srsltid=AfmBOoruGUoc3m_kUsDNIpyMPEdVwJC_lu3I6PTScm46z4VanildP4Fb

Williams, N. (2024). 10 Essential Elements for Creating Harmony in Relationships. Marriage.com. https://www.marriage.com/advice/relationship/harmony-in-relationship/

www.wisdomlib.org. (2024, September 20). Microcosm and macrocosm: Significance and symbolism. Wisdomlib.org. https://www.wisdomlib.org/concept/microcosm-and-macrocosm

Zimmerman, E. (2018, August 3). The Three Life-Altering Benefits of Journaling - Elle Zimmerman. Ellezimmerman.com. https://ellezimmerman.com/life-altering-benefits-journaling/

Image Sources

1 https://commons.wikimedia.org/wiki/File:Nile_River_Delta_(MODIS_2022-07-19).jpg
2 Eternal Space, CC BY-SA 4.0 <https://creativecommons.org/licenses/by-sa/4.0>, via Wikimedia Commons.
https://commons.wikimedia.org/wiki/File:Maat_(Goddess).png
3 WSP300, CC0, via Wikimedia Commons.
https://commons.wikimedia.org/wiki/File:Ancient_Egyptian_Vexilloids_in_Tomb_Paintings_1.webp
4 Jeff Dahl, CC BY-SA 4.0 <https://creativecommons.org/licenses/by-sa/4.0>, via Wikimedia Commons. https://commons.wikimedia.org/wiki/File:Re-Horakhty.svg
5 Jeff Dahl, CC BY-SA 4.0 <https://creativecommons.org/licenses/by-sa/4.0>, via Wikimedia Commons.
https://commons.wikimedia.org/wiki/File:Standing_Osiris.svg
6 EternalSpace1977, CC BY-SA 4.0 <https://creativecommons.org/licenses/by-sa/4.0>, via Wikimedia Commons.
https://commons.wikimedia.org/wiki/File:Isis_(goddess).png
7 Eternal Space, CC BY-SA 4.0 <https://creativecommons.org/licenses/by-sa/4.0>, via Wikimedia Commons. https://commons.wikimedia.org/wiki/File:Set_(God).png
8 No machine-readable author provided. Jeff Dahl assumed (based on copyright claims). CC BY-SA 4.0 <https://creativecommons.org/licenses/by-sa/4.0>, via Wikimedia Commons. https://commons.wikimedia.org/wiki/File:Maat.svg
9 https://commons.wikimedia.org/wiki/File:Egypt_dauingevekten.jpg
10 Jeff Dahl, CC0, via Wikimedia Commons.
https://commons.wikimedia.org/wiki/File:Feather_of_maat.svg

11 Designed by Freepik, https://www.freepik.com/free-vector/gradient-numerology-background_37573680.htm

12 Designed by Freepik, https://www.freepik.com/free-photo/fantasy-astral-wallpaper-composition_39425675.htm

13 AmosWolfe, Jeff Dahl, CC0, via Wikimedia Commons. https://commons.wikimedia.org/wiki/File:Ankh_and_Eye_of_Horus.svg

14 No machine-readable author provided. Amos Wolfe assumed (based on copyright claims). Public domain, via Wikimedia Commons. https://commons.wikimedia.org/wiki/File:Ankh.svg

15 Jeff Dahl, CC BY-SA 4.0 <https://creativecommons.org/licenses/by-sa/4.0>, via Wikimedia Commons. https://commons.wikimedia.org/wiki/File:Eye_of_Horus_bw.svg

16 Lorc, CC BY 3.0 <https://creativecommons.org/licenses/by/3.0>, via Wikimedia Commons. https://commons.wikimedia.org/wiki/File:Scarab-beetle_-_Lorc_-_game-icons.svg

17 Metropolitan Museum of Art, CC0, via Wikimedia Commons https://commons.wikimedia.org/wiki/File:Djed_Pillar_Amulet_MET_90.6.226_FRONT.jpeg

18 Designed by Freepik, https://www.freepik.com/free-photo/freedom-concept-with-woman-holding-cloth-nature_4627798.htm

19 Image by svklimkin from Pixabay https://pixabay.com/photos/flower-life-yellow-flower-crack-887443/

20 Image by PublicDomainPictures from Pixabay https://pixabay.com/photos/grass-lawn-grass-blades-grassy-275986/

21 Image by Michaela from Pixabay https://pixabay.com/photos/a-book-pages-read-training-novel-5178205/

22 Image by DaveMeier from Pixabay https://pixabay.com/photos/tree-trunk-roots-bark-tree-trunk-569275/

23 Image by StockSnap from Pixabay https://pixabay.com/photos/writing-writer-notes-pen-notebook-923882/

www.ingramcontent.com/pod-product-compliance
Lightning Source LLC
Chambersburg PA
CBHW051849160426
43209CB00006B/1219